# WANDERINGS IN WALES

Roads

Authors Route shown thus

Miles  0     10     20

BRISTOL CHANNEL

Newport

CARDIFF

Abergavenny

Skirrid Fawr
Skirrid Fach
Sugar Loaf
Llanthony Priory
Crickhowell
CASTELL DINAS
WAUN FACH
BLACK MTS

Builth Wells

DRYGARN FAWR

Brecon

Llandovery

CARREG DU
BRYNTEG
PEN-Y-FAN
FAN FAWR
BRECON BEACONS
Merthyr Tydfil
CARMARTHEN VAN
FAN GIHIRYCH
FAN HIR
R. Neath
R. Tawe

Bridgend

SWANSEA
Oystermouth Castle
Mumbles
Langland Bay
Caswell Bay
Brandy Cove
Pwll-du-Head
Penard Castle
Three Cliffs Bay

Llanelly

CEFN-Y-BRYN
Bishopston

LLANMADOC HILL
Rhossily
Newslade Bay
Port Eynon
Oxwich

Llandilo

Carmarthen

St. Clears

Cardigan

Fishguard

Preselly Hills

Haverfordwest

Milford Haven

Pembroke

Carew
Lydstep
Penally
Tenby
CALDEY I.

Manorbier
Sprinkle Haven

Stack Rocks
Saddle Head
Stackpole Estate
ST. GOVAN'S HEAD

D0537169

# WANDERINGS IN
# WALES

# W.A. POUCHER

# WANDERINGS IN WALES

## WANDERINGS IN WALES

One of the chief attractions of this book is that it covers much more than the familiar beauty spots in Wales. Mr Poucher has made it a special object to explore the comparatively little-known inland counties of Radnor and Brecknock, and the results of his quest will surprise those to whom this region is new as much as they will delight those who know it already.

'Not only are his photographs well up to his usual fine standard, but his commentary on them, in the form of a journal of his four months' wandering from the Bristol Channel coast to Anglesey, gives details which will be most useful to those readers of his book (and they will be many) who want to explore the little-visited glories he reveals in his pictures.'

*Birmingham Post*

'Many books have been written about the beauty of Wales but most authors have been content to keep to the beaten track. Mr W. A. Poucher has been visiting Wales for 25 years and in his new book he gives us glimpses of more remote corners. Over 200 magnificent photographs by the author provide a pictorial record of his tour and make the reader want to become better acquainted with the scenes depicted. Mr Poucher has weighed the claims of each district and the attractiveness of South Wales as a holiday centre has not for once been overshadowed by the allurement of North Wales.'

*Western Mail*

*By the Same Author*

ESCAPE TO THE HILLS
THE BACKBONE OF ENGLAND
LAKELAND THROUGH THE LENS
SNOWDONIA THROUGH THE LENS
SCOTLAND THROUGH THE LENS
LAKELAND HOLIDAY
SNOWDON HOLIDAY
HIGHLAND HOLIDAY
LAKELAND JOURNEY
PEAK PANORAMA
A CAMERA IN THE CAIRNGORMS
OVER LAKELAND FELLS
THE MAGIC OF SKYE

SPRINKLE HAVEN, LYDSTEP

# WANDERINGS IN WALES

By W. A. POUCHER, F.R.P.S.

WITH PHOTOGRAPHS
BY THE AUTHOR

LONDON: COUNTRY LIFE LIMITED

2-10 TAVISTOCK STREET, COVENT GARDEN, W.C. 2

TO

RICHARD BALCOMB
NORMAN TAYLOR
ROBERT TYSSEN-GEE
GOOD COMPANIONS ON THESE WANDERINGS

*First published 1949*

*Printed in Great Britain by*
*Billing and Sons Ltd., Guildford and Esher*
17607

# PREFACE

Wales is often looked upon as a wild and sombre country whose mineral wealth has been exploited by industrialists to such an extent that its landscape is disfigured by mine workings, and its atmosphere polluted with the smoke of factory chimneys.

While this may be true of certain areas in South Wales, many of its seaside resorts are so attractive that they have for years been frequented by thousands of holiday-makers, and the mountains of Snowdonia are so captivating that they also have become the playground of legions of rock-climbers and hill-walkers. These districts, however, form a relatively small part of the great Principality, and much of the rest of it still awaits the coming of the tourist in search of scenes of fresh beauty.

The reason for this apparent lack of appreciation may be due to the fact that the excellence of Welsh scenery as a whole has never been fully disclosed to the traveller, either by publicity or by a camera artist who has perceived its real charm.

In these circumstances I set off on these wanderings, my object being to explore and photograph its unknown beauty. I therefore chose a route that would encompass the best of its glorious seascapes and historic castles, as well as the most unfrequented of its lonely mountains and valleys.

Readers who turn the pages of this book will perhaps be surprised to find that it reveals scenes of unexpected splendour, and I hope it will induce them to forsake their favourite haunts for at least one holiday, even if they follow in my footsteps for only a part of these wanderings.

The present industrial revolution includes a great expansion of holidays, and it will create thousands of new wayfarers who should be offered every inducement to spend them in Wales. In selecting this fine country they will not only be rewarded by fresh air, healthy exercise, and every variety of beauty, but they will also relieve the pressure on existing popular centres where hotel accommodation is already totally inadequate to meet present needs, let alone those of the future.

COURTLANDS,                                             W. A. POUCHER.
KINGSWOOD,
SURREY.

# CONTENTS

(*Plates are referred to in italic type*)

# CONTENTS

7

# CONTENTS

# The Charm of Wales

The strange beauty of North Wales is known to thousands of visitors and is appreciated especially by all those who love wild and grand scenery. It has always appealed to me strongly, and in consequence I have visited this mountainous district regularly during the past twenty-five years. I have scaled its shapely peaks, tramped its desolate valleys, explored its savage cwms, and spent countless hours in solitude beside its remote and lonely tarns. Throughout the years these precious experiences have constantly evoked happy memories, not only of the country itself, but also of the many kindly folk I have met there. Indeed, I have been so fascinated by this incomparable landscape that I have already described and portrayed much of it in three previous volumes.

This area forms a relatively small part of Wales, but it embraces the most picturesque hills which are huddled round Snowdon, the highest peak in this country. These rugged mountains have now become a popular playground for the rock-climber, every crag has been explored minutely by experts, and the innumerable courses which festoon them all have been accurately described and indexed for the guidance of these sportsmen.

The whole of the Principality, however, is mountainous, and both South- and Mid-Wales display several groups of hills that merit the attention of the climber: the graceful Brecon Beacons are prominent in the former area, and the massive and precipitous Cader Idris in the latter. Although this fine mountain is not the highest in Central Wales it completely dominates the district, and its remarkable topography has for years attracted the hill-walker, whereas, for one reason or another, it has been deserted by the rock-climber.

It was only in the past decade that I fully realised the possibilities of these parts of Wales as an alternative venue for the wayfarer, and while the aforementioned groups are the most outstanding there are many other interesting hills which frown upon the vast stretches of billowy moorland that encompass them all. These treasured solitudes are comparatively unknown and unexplored and still await the coming of the tourist, who may walk over them at high level for days on end without meeting another human being, save perhaps the occasional shepherd tending his flock. Heather and bent deck this wonderful landscape, tracks are few and far between, but the whole of it is enlivened by the glint of light on the little tarns and innumerable pools that are splashed about everywhere.

This upland medley is threaded by a variety of valleys that range from the spacious, sweeping glens, dotted with farmsteads and patterned with fields, to the wild and narrow defiles which often terminate in lofty and savage divides. Many of them carry well-engineered roads that provide the main lines of communication between the adjacent areas. Others are penetrated by sinuous cart-tracks whose traverse may well become an adventure for the motorist. Some of these thoroughfares end deep in the heads of grand cwms where further progress must of necessity be made on foot, whereas a few of them twist and turn treacherously as they ascend the steep hill-sides, finally to cross the passes into the next valleys. The extraordinary narrowness of some of the latter, especially where they lead into the fastnesses of the higher hills, should be a warning to drivers to be on the look-out for any eventuality, for it is frequently impossible to find a passing place and in consequence it may be necessary to reverse a long distance should another vehicle be encountered. However, these risky routes are usually left severely alone by owners who have any respect for their cars. In a few instances the highways rise along the enclosing flanks of the valleys and reveal a kaleidoscopic panorama of entrancing beauty as the traveller gains height. A remarkable example of this sort is the Rheidol Valley in Mid-Wales, which terminates in a gigantic wooded basin at the Devil's Bridge: it affords perhaps the most spectacular scene in the Principality.

Wales, like every other mountainous district in Britain, is resplendent with lakes. Some of them have exquisite settings, while others are bosomed amid a wilderness of rock and scree. Several are situated beside main roads and thus are observed in one of their many moods by every passing traveller. As a rule their environs are not so well wooded as those of English Lakeland or the Scottish Highlands, but nevertheless they display a rare beauty that appeals to all who see them.

It is, however, the remote and less well-known sheets of water that disclose the real charms of this country. They are reached only by those wayfarers who are bent upon a search for beauty, and are often cradled on lofty ridges which reveal striking panoramas of the engirdling scene. Some of the lakes have been converted into gigantic reservoirs, and while such metamorphoses are frequently deplored by lovers of wild scenery it must be admitted that many of them enhance the prospect in parts of this desolate landscape.

Those who enjoy fishing will find plenty of trout in the lakes and tarns, and anglers' hotels are sprinkled about the whole country; some are situated on the very edges of the lakes, and others within easy access of them.

Stately rivers, tumultuous streams, and glittering cascades appeal to everyone, and all Wales is rich in these features. Some of them have been over-praised, but a few which are found in remote parts of the country have not received the approbation they deserve. Height and volume are not necessarily the sole attributes of a waterfall; setting and environs also add charm, and it is here that Wales rises above comparable British scenery.

The coastline of the Principality presents an immense contrast to the inland uplands, and the greater part of it is well known to legions of visitors. Such places as Llandudno, Rhyl, and Aberystwyth need no praise from me, but the surprising thing about this long and varied seascape is that its finest sections in the south are comparatively unknown. This may not be entirely true of the Gower peninsula, which lies so near to the great industrial city of Swansea, because its inhabitants have every opportunity of walking over it at week-ends, but the fact remains that the magnificent coast of Pembrokeshire is scarcely noticed by many holiday-makers at such nearby resorts as Tenby. I stayed there in the course of these wanderings and to my astonishment chatted with several visitors who had never heard of the remarkable beauty of Lydstep Caverns, let alone the superlative grandeur of the coastline further to the west.

This apparent neglect may be due to the fact that the majority of summer visitors like a lazy holiday and prefer merely to bathe or to sit on the sands in the warm sunshine, rather than to go farther afield in search of beauty. The coastline is a long one and a car is necessary for its thorough exploration, but Lydstep is quite near to Tenby and may be easily reached on foot. I hope that readers may be tempted to go there, when they will be delighted with the spectacular limestone cliffs that enclose the wild little coves.

The Castles of Wales are famous, and the wonders of such grand edifices as Caernarvon and Harlech have a world-wide reputation. They are viewed by thousands of visitors annually, whereas many of those fortresses in the south that thrust their gaunt, ruined battlements into the sky are never seen except by the antiquary. These magnificent relics of the past glories of Wales merit greater attention by the tourist and should be inspected by all those staying in the vicinity.

THE SNOWDON RAILWAY

# The People

This brief description of Wales would be sadly incomplete without some mention of its people. It is well known that about half the population is concentrated in the iron- and coal-bearing valley of Glamorgan, that the whole race is hardy, and that they are very musical. In addition, most of them are bi-lingual and prefer to converse among themselves in their own Celtic tongue. When travellers go to Wales for the first time they are apt to notice this peculiarity, which gives them the illusion of being in a foreign country, and it may be for this reason that a few of them have expressed a dislike for the natives. My frequent visits to this country have given me a great liking for the Welsh, for I have found them friendly, kindly, and considerate; willing to advise me on any problem that may arise during my sojourn there; and at all times most courteous and entertaining.

The object of my wanderings has been primarily a search for beauty rather than a study of character, although the latter is inevitably associated with it to a greater or lesser degree, and is, moreover, a factor that cannot be ignored by any observant traveller. I have therefore never devoted as much time to the people themselves as did George Borrow in his famous journey through their country, but I have always chatted with those I have encountered and invariably found their conversation illuminating and interesting. Moreover, I have discovered the farmers to be especially helpful, and they have always been most willing to give me, not only access to their lands, but also advice about the best routes to any of the hills near their farmsteads.

Accommodation in Wales is usually on a generous scale, and especially so on the coast. In the northern mountain districts hotels and inns are dotted about at convenient points within easy reach of all the well-known ascents, and to a lesser degree this also applies to the hill districts in the south. In Mid-Wales, however, all the groups other than Cader Idris are situated at considerable distances from the hotel centres, and in consequence they are not easily reached without transport. When I have been travelling on foot in these areas I have found the hotel proprietors most helpful and even anxious to assist me by providing a car on occasion to take me to some distant place, which has saved miles of foot-slogging on hard and uninteresting roads and, incidentally, allowed more time for the exhilarating walks on the hills.

THE OLD COW INN, ABERGAVENNY

# The Weather

When people take a holiday they immediately become concerned about the weather, although while they are at home, or at business, atmospheric conditions are of less interest and frequently escape them. Like all mountainous country the Welsh hills collect clouds which are often precipitated as rain, and in consequence the risk of bad weather is always present. After many years' experience in the British Hills I have come to the conclusion that, on average, Wales is neither better nor worse than any of the other mountainous districts which are adjacent to the western coast of our islands. Fine and wet spells come and go, and it is entirely a matter of luck whether the traveller strikes one or other of these conditions when he takes his holiday.

I have found spring the best time for good weather anywhere in Britain, and those who are able to get away would be well advised to take their vacations at that time of year. Of course, by doing so they will miss the pageantry of autumn, but they will find compensation in the freshness of the trees and the brightness of the wild flowers which at this season carpet the fields and woods. Those who go to the sea, however, will find less hazardous conditions at any time of year, for I have frequently seen the coastline of Wales bathed in brilliant sunlight when the hills immediately behind it have been shrouded in cloud and rain. This point is admirably illustrated by the accompanying photograph. The farm in the foreground is situated on the hillside just above Caernarvon, and the coast in the vicinity basked in the sun all day, whereas the piling cumulus in the background completely enveloped all the mountains of Snowdonia. Beneath that canopy all the hills were black and forbidding in the dim light, and the rain was so heavy that climbing became an unpleasant and unrewarding experience. In any case my advice is "Go to Wales and explore its wonderful landscape." If you want to take advantage of the best weather stay at a seaside resort, and when the hills at the back are clear, go and climb them.

A FARM IN THE WELSH HILLS

# Glossary of Welsh Place-Names

When I first went to Wales I found it difficult to understand the meanings of the various Welsh names given to the different topographical features of the district. I hope, therefore, the translation of some of them as set out below will be useful to travellers in this delectable country.

*Aber*, a river mouth.
*Ach*, water.
*Afon*, a river.
*Allt*, a wooded slope.
*Aran*, a high place.
*Bach*, little.
*Bala*, an outlet.
*Ber*, a hill top.
*Bettws*, a chapel.
*Blaen*, the head of a valley.
*Bont*, a bridge.
*Braich*, an arm.
*Bron*, the slope of a hill.
*Bryn*, a mound or hill.
*Bwlch*, a pass.
*Bychan*, small.
*Cader*, a chair.
*Cae*, an enclosed field.
*Caer*, a camp or fortress.
*Careg*, a rock or stone.
*Carn*, a cairn or heap of stones.
*Capel*, a chapel.
*Carnedd*, a cairn.
*Castell*, a castle or fortress.
*Cefn*, a ridge.
*Clogwyn*, a cliff or precipice.
*Coch*, red.
*Coed*, a wood.
*Cors*, a bog.
*Craig*, a crag or rock.
*Croes*, a cross.
*Crib*, a ridge or jagged edge.
*Crug*, a mound.
*Cwm*, a hollow.
*Cymmer*, a junction or confluence.
*Dinas*, a natural fortress.
*Drws*, a gate.
*Du*, black.
*Dyffryn*, a wide valley.
*Esgair*, a long ridge.
*Fach*, little.
*Fan*, a high place.
*Fawr*, large.

*Foel*, a bare hill.
*Ffynnon*, a well or spring.
*Gaer*, a camp.
*Garth*, a hill or headland.
*Gallt*, a slope.
*Glas*, blue or green.
*Glyn*, a glen.
*Goch*, red.
*Gribin*, a little ridge.
*Hafod*, a summer dwelling.
*Hen*, old.
*Llan*, a church.
*Llech*, a flat stone.
*Llwyd*, grey.
*Llyn*, a lake.
*Maes*, a field.
*Mawr*, great.
*Moel*, a bare rounded hill.
*Mynydd*, a mountain.
*Mynach*, a monk.
*Morfa*, a marsh by the sea.
*Nant*, a brook.
*Ogof*, a cave.
*Pant*, a hollow.
*Pen*, a head, peak, or top.
*Pentre*, a village.
*Pont*, a bridge.
*Porth*, a port, gate, or harbour.
*Pistyll*, a waterfall.
*Plas*, a place or mansion.
*Pwll*, a pool.
*Rhaiadr*, a cataract.
*Rhiw*, a slope.
*Rhudd*, reddish.
*Rhyd*, a ford.
*Sarn*, a causeway.
*Sych*, dry.
*Tal*, brow of hill.
*Tomen*, a mound.
*Tref*, a dwelling.
*Ty*, a house.
*Uchaf*, higher.
*Y—Yr*, the.

# The Black Mountains

The Black Mountains cover an area of about 80 square miles to the north of Abergavenny. They consist largely of bleak, whale-back ridges running from south-east to north-west, and are dominated by the Gader Ridge, which is crowned by Waun Fach, the highest peak in the whole group. Strangely enough all of them are of about the same altitude, and rise just above the 2,000-foot contour, but Waun Fach is a conspicuous grassy hump whose cairn is 2,660 feet above sea level.

Three long valleys penetrate the fastnesses of the range: the Vale of Ewyas is the longest and most beautiful and is graced by the venerable ruin of Llanthony Priory. All the valleys follow roughly parallel lines in a north-westerly direction and terminate in the shadow of a broken ridge which connects all four of the main ridges.

Abergavenny is often spoken of as the "Gateway of Wales," and indeed this description is most apt when the town is seen from Skirrid Fach, a small eminence that stands to the east of it and from which can be seen the houses clustered together between the prominent cone of the Sugar Loaf to the north and the massive hill of Blorenge to the south, the fair land of Wales being clearly revealed to the west between these lofty portals. Skirrid Fawr is another conspicuous hill in the vicinity; moreover, the town is a convenient centre for the exploration of the Black Mountains.

Abergavenny is situated on the River Usk, at the confluence of the Gavenny from which it takes its name. The hotels are patronised largely by trout and salmon fishermen, but there are other attractions besides fishing, for the Roman remains draw the antiquaries, who, however, are not agreed as to whether the town is the modern counterpart of the Roman *Gobanvium*. The Castle is an interesting structure: it was founded soon after the Norman Conquest, but its remnants belong to the fourteenth century. It stands well above the green fields which border the Usk and affords a pleasant venue for an evening promenade.

In view of these numerous attractions I decided to begin my *Wanderings in Wales* by climbing all the hills in the district, and arrived at Abergavenny during a heat wave early in April. It was uncomfortably hot in the town owing to its enclosed position, and on the first day I tried to find some fresh air by ascending Skirrid Fawr. The summit is four miles away and, at a height of only 1,601 feet, dominates a ridge about a mile in length, of which 200 acres were presented to the National Trust by Major J. Herbert. The road passes near its lower end, so I parked my car here and crossed the adjacent fields which give access to the ridge. It took me only twenty minutes to attain it, but when I breasted the final slope not a breath of air stirred, and the Black Mountains were dimmed by an almost impenetrable haze. Under a cloudless sky I wandered slowly along the crest of the ridge, which is broad and grassy, with here and there a small outcrop of rock to break its undulations. At the last of them I first perceived the precipitous façade of red sandstone which flanks the western aspect of the summit and, according to tradition, is the result of a great landslide that occurred on the night of the Crucifixion—hence the name "Holy Mountain."

A few minutes later I was sitting on top of the hill, where I lazed away a couple of hours in the stifling heat. I knew full well, however, that I should have to return on another day if I was to secure the photographs merited by its position, which is immediately opposite the Sugar Loaf and the principal mountain group. In the afternoon I examined the shattered precipice below the summit and found it to be the nesting-place of legions of crows: it would offer little sport for the climber. Large quantities of scree lay below in a little valley which is enclosed by a small subsidiary ridge.

It was just as sultry next day, but since the atmosphere was clearer I walked up to the Sugar Loaf. This conical hill is four miles from the town and I approached the open ground below it by way of Chapel Road. A field path then leads to a farm and some cottages nestling at the foot of Rholben, one of the subsidiary ridges of the peak. Ascending the steep grassy track flanked with glowing dead bracken, I soon attained its crest and then followed a dilapidated stone wall where many a wind-blown larch leaned over to the north-east. The trees extended for about a mile, and I afterwards passed a newly planted copse of similar trees on my right before attacking the final slopes of the Sugar Loaf. I kept to the spongy turf path, and, after climbing a short distance, found a stream of delicious cold water where I thankfully quenched my thirst. The last 100 feet is steep, but I soon reached the outcrop of yellow sandstone which marks the eastern end of the 300-yard long summit ridge. The ridge is narrow and carries an O.S. Triangulation Station at the highest point in its centre, where it is 1,955 feet high. A refreshing

*(Continued on page 24.)*

ABERGAVENNY CASTLE

THE SUGAR LOAF FROM ABERGAVENNY

THE SUGAR LOAF FROM RHOLBEN

BLORENGE FROM ABERGAVENNY

ABERGAVENNY AND SKIRRID FAWR FROM BLORENGE

19

THE ABBEY HOTEL, LLANTHONY

LLANTHONY PRIORY

SKIRRID FAWR

THE SUMMIT OF SKIRRID FAWR

## THE BLACK MOUNTAINS. (*Continued from page 14.*)

breeze was blowing, I discovered a comfortable seat and, while eating my sandwiches, admired the extensive panorama which includes the Gader Ridge and all the outliers already mentioned.

The April summer continued and next afternoon I walked up Skirrid Fach. It is only 886 feet high and is reached by a track from the Great Western Railway Station. The summit is small, girt with trees, and covered with the softest of green turf. I was sorry, however, to see that much of it had been wantonly damaged, presumably by young lovers, who evidently had nothing better to do than to cut their initials centrally in a number of hearts!

The day I was waiting for dawned eventually. It had rained all night, the temperature had fallen, and the north-west wind of the morning brought fine cumulus which dappled a purple sky. I was about early, and, immediately after breakfast, set off in my car for Llanthony Priory, eleven miles away. The enchanting drive up the sequestered Vale of Ewyas took me right into the heart of the Black Mountains, where the fresh green of the larches, backed by the barren hills and a glorious

sky, made a changing picture of infinite beauty. The Priory is a fine old ruin: it was an Augustinian Monastery and was founded at the beginning of the twelfth century. Much of it is in good condition, but parts have been converted into the Abbey Hotel. Peace and solitude reigned supreme in this remote spot, which is frequented mainly by fishermen and, occasionally, by hill walkers.

I was so delighted with this restful scene that I could have lingered here all day, but after wandering in the vicinity for an hour I regretfully left it behind, for I had much to do while conditions were propitious. I made for Skirrid Fawr again, and in a couple of hours had traversed the ridge, photographed everything of note, and returned to my car. From there I went to Skirrid Fach and was back again in an hour. To complete the exploits of the day I drove through Abergavenny and then up the steep, twisting road to Bleanavon, but left my car at the Keeper's Pool, a small sheet of water lying in a hollow at 1,583 feet near the crest of the pass. I walked over Blorenge, following the green path below its crest on the outward journey,

MOUNTAINS FROM SKIRRID FAWR

and returning over the two summits which are 1,832 feet above sea level. The views from the path were more revealing than those from the slightly higher tops, and disclosed Abergavenny far below backed by Skirrid Fawr, together with every other eminence in the district.

The good weather continued, so next day I packed my bags and drove along the road through Crickhowell and Tretower, to leave my car eventually at the tiny hamlet of Pen-y-Genffarodd, which stands on the crest of the pass. I found all the inhabitants dressed in their Sunday best and slowly wending their way to church. I was bound for the Gader Ridge and asked some of them if they could direct me to it, but, alas, none of them had ever heard of it! However, my trusty map indicated the ascent of Y Grib as the key to its discovery, so I set off by walking along an old farm track which led towards it. Passing round the north side of Castell Dinas, I deserted the farm road and took a direct line for the end of the spur that rose into the sky ahead. I found the ridge surprisingly narrow, with sharp undulations, and adorned here and there with prominent outcrops of rock. As I gained height the fresh north-west

wind acted like wine and I swung along almost unconscious of the steep rises as they followed one another in quick succession. Sheep were grazing everywhere, and here and there I espied a fell pony enjoying the freedom of the hills.

In an hour and a half I stood on the broad grassy top of Pen-y-Manllwyn, which is the northern outpost of the Gader Ridge. Turning to the south I kept to its crest, first climbing to the O.S. Triangulation Station, which revealed the strange hump of Waun Fach another mile to the south. I picked my way carefully across the intervening boggy ground and finally stood by the cairn, which disclosed an immense panorama with the Brecon Beacons as the most prominent objects on the distant skyline and the great whale-back ridges of the Black Mountains immediately below blocking out all views of the deep valleys of the range. The wind was terrific on this lofty belvedere and it was bitterly cold in spite of the brilliant sunshine. In these circumstances I ate a hurried lunch and then retraced my steps, meeting two other trampers only on this delectable day on the comparatively unknown hills of Wales.

THE GADER RIDGE FROM NEAR TRETOWER

Y GRIB LEADING TO PEN-Y-MANLLWYN

THE BRECON BEACONS FROM Y GRIB

28

WAUN FACH AND THE SUGAR LOAF FROM THE NORTH

# The Brecon Beacons

The Brecon Beacons are strung out across the skyline about mid-way between the Black Mountains on the east and the Black Mountain (Carmarthen Van) on the west. The principal summits in this long line of hills are spread over a distance of some 10 miles, and are, from east to west: Pen-y-Fan, 2,907 feet; Fan Fawr, 2,409 feet; Fan Llia, 2,071 feet; Fan Nedd, 2,177 feet; and Fan Gihirych, 2,381 feet. Pen-y-Fan is the loftiest peak in South Wales and forms a conspicuous object when seen from afar. Actually it comprises three summits very close together: Bryn Teg, 2,608 feet, rising to the east of the reigning peak, and Carn Du, 2,863 feet, on its west. They make an attractive mountain group when viewed from the north, and the dominating peak assumes spectacular proportions when seen from the adjacent rib of Bryn Teg. Pen-y-Fan is five miles to the south-west of Brecon.

On the completion of my walk over the Gader Ridge I motored to the county town of Brecon with the object of climbing the Beacons. It rained the day after my arrival, but I sallied forth to explore the country to the south because, when the weather favoured an ascent, I wished to approach as near as possible to Pen-y-Fan by car. I was most anxious to have a clear idea of its topography, for my previous experiences of Welsh mountain roads had been none too happy. I did not want to damage or bog my vehicle merely to save a mile or two of foot-slogging. I crossed the bridge over the River Usk and turned off the highway to the left at a church, following the rising road, which, according to the map, led to the farm of Pant (a hollow place or valley). Although this road is shown on the map as a mere line, I found it narrow but well surfaced. After walking about three miles I discovered a place below Pant where I could turn the car safely and so returned to my hotel.

Next morning I woke to find the sunlight streaming in at my window and fine clouds sailing by in a blue sky, so, after an early breakfast, I drove straight to my parking place. At 9.30 a.m. I was changing into nailed boots and, on donning my rucksack and cameras, was gratified to see broken masses of cumulus passing over the summit of Pen-y-Fan, driven by a north-east wind. I advanced along the by-way which soon deteriorated into a stony cart track. It crossed a brook fringed with trees and then began to climb steeply towards the head of Cwm Cynwyn.

There was perhaps a mile of this sinuous, canopied road, and then a gate gave access to the open hill-side. Deserting the road I bore to the right and climbed the grassy slopes leading to the broad ridge ahead. These proved to be longer than I had anticipated and I must have proceeded for a mile before the sharp rib of Bryn Teg came into view. A few pools were dotted about the long crest of the ridge, which seemed completely devoid of rock. Far below, on my left, the cart track twisted and turned as it rose gradually to the pass between the hills, and in front of me a long ridge swept up from it to end at the summit of Bryn Teg. The northern flanks of this hill were exceedingly steep, and much of the grass had been carried away by a landslide so that the red rocky soil beneath was revealed. A little col further to the right separated the hill from Pen-y-Fan, whose face, seamed with gullies hundreds of feet long, and ribbed with grass and moss, swept down precipitously to the stream which had its source in the hollow between the two peaks.

I climbed the *arête* of Bryn Teg, and when about half-way up espied two people standing on the summit of the reigning peak. As I reached the top they came to meet me and in the course of our conversation said they were staying at the Youth Hostel near the Storey Arms, which is situated to the west of Pen-y-Fan.

The descent to the col was a delight, with the riven façade of the giant mountain facing me all the time, and I kept to the edge of the precipices because they afforded some fine foregrounds for photographs. The wind was terrific at the col, which acted like a gigantic funnel, but I crossed it easily and climbed the ridge towards my lofty goal.

On approaching the summit I noticed that its flat top was supported by blocks of red sandstone lying end-on and poised high above the innumerable horizontal layers of the same material, which alternated with successive bands of bright red earth. Although I carefully examined these precipices, I could not imagine their offering any serious sport for the rock-climber, for not only were they very steep, but also the shattered face appeared to be in an advanced state of disintegration.

In a short time I stood on the little summit plateau which carries an O.S. Triangulation Station, and afterwards passed it on my way to Carn Du. A high col separates the two peaks, and in a few minutes I was striding across the flat top of the latter to look down

PEN-Y-FAN FROM PANT

upon the road far below backed by the line of Beacons which terminated with Carmarthen Van in the far distance. The atmosphere had been clear up to mid-day, but the north-east wind brought haze, and when I returned to Pen-y-Fan the great mass of the Black Mountains to the east had been completely obscured by it. I sat down in a sheltered spot to eat my sandwiches and revelled in the solitude and silence of the mountain-top while enjoying such of the extensive panorama as I could see.

After lazing away an hour I left it all behind to descend the broad grassy ridge of Cefn-cwm-llwch, which is the usual route of ascent from Pant. I passed through the little farmstead, chatted with the farmer for a few moments, and then walked down to my car, the descent having taken one and a quarter hours only.

BRYN TEG—2,608 FEET HIGH

PEN-Y-FAN—2,907 FEET HIGH

PEN-Y-FAN FROM BRYN TEG

THE SUMMIT OF PEN-Y-FAN

CARN DU FROM PEN-Y-FAN

LLYN CWM LLWCH FROM CARN DU

# The Elan Valley

The Elan Valley lies some three miles to the west of Rhayader, a charming town standing astride the River Wye, and is engirdled by rounded hills that rise to a height of about 2,000 feet. The floor of the valley is occupied by three reservoirs which supply water to the city of Birmingham. The works were begun in 1893, and were opened by King Edward VII and Queen Alexandra on July 21st, 1904.

The area of the watershed, the highest point of which is 2,115 feet, is over 71 square miles. Of this area 20,515 acres drain into the Elan Valley, and 25,047 acres into the adjacent Claerwen. The calculated average rainfall in the former is 68·8 inches. The aqueduct starts from the Careg-ddu reservoir and is situated at a height of 770 feet near the viaduct, which spans a submerged dam. It conveys the water to Frankley Storage Reservoir, over 73 miles away, with a fall of only 170 feet. Since this reservoir is nearly seven miles from Birmingham, the water is conveyed a total distance of approximately 80 miles, which is about 5 miles further than that from Lake Vyrnwy to Liverpool, and about 15 miles shorter than that from Thirlmere to Manchester.

The full water scheme for Birmingham includes three dams in the Claerwen Valley, but their construction has been postponed until an increased supply is required.

The Elan Valley is known to thousands and its beauty is almost legendary. I had never visited it, so took the opportunity of doing so while staying in Brecon. It is equally accessible from Aberystwyth, but the water-play in any valley is one of its chief attractions and, if it is to be seen at its best, the valley must be ascended, so that it is ahead during the advance.

I left my hotel on a sunny morning when the north-east wind brought cloud, accompanied by some haze. I drove across country to join the upper valley of the Wye, and, while ascending it in the direction of Builth Wells, stopped frequently to admire its lovely scenery. Some sections of the tree-girt river took wide sweeping bends between the gently sloping hills and were enlivened by tiny cascades that sparkled in the sunlight as they swept over the innumerable flat rocky ledges forming the bed of the stream. In these places the water was low, and in consequence there were many little craggy pools, some of them bare and others green with mosses, while everywhere lichened boulders lent variety to the scene. In other sections, where the river was deep, the water flowed slowly and its placid surface often reflected a white-washed farmstead perched on the opposite bank.

Beside these peaceful stretches, sheep with their newly born lambs loitered to nibble the succulent grass.

The road leaves the river to the north of Builth Wells, but returns to it at Newbridge-on-Wye and then follows a sinuous course on its left bank as far as Rhayader. The bare brown hills increase in stature as one advances and culminate in the rounded top of Drygarn Fawr, a height of 2,115 feet, some ten miles to the west of Newbridge. There was little traffic on this road, so I proceeded at a leisurely pace and was thus able to scan the increasingly beautiful landscape without leaving my car.

At Rhayader I turned to the left, crossed the bridge over the Wye, and for three miles followed a south-westerly course beside the Afon Elan. The road must have been improved in recent years, because a water-splash referred to in the guidebooks as being near the Elan Valley Hotel has now disappeared. The hills close in after some two and a half miles, the road steepens, and then, on rounding a bend, the first dam comes into view. The landscape here is rather barren, and as the water in the first reservoir was not high enough to overflow the dam, the scene lost much of its charm. I stopped for a few minutes to look at it, and then continued for half a mile, to leave my car at the viaduct. This is a delightful spot: the hill to the west is shagged with trees with a small church in their midst, while the Foel Valve Tower housing the aqueduct intake is just round the corner, and from it can be seen a long stretch of the Careg-ddu Reservoir to the north, hemmed in by frowning crags and fringed with trees.

I left the road and, descending to the water's edge, walked along the grassy banks. The prospect was very lovely: the soft green track in the turf; the murmur of the water lapping the shore below; the glitter of sunlight on its rippling surface; dainty birches with their delicate branches swaying in the breeze; tufts of yellow primroses here and there; the glow of immense patches of golden gorse on the hillsides; and a glorious sky overhead in which fine clouds sailed gaily along. I could easily have spent the day in this enchanting place where I seemed to be the sole human being, but, having much more of the long valley to see, I returned to my car and followed the road northwards.

This excellently constructed highway bends sharply to the left at the end of the first reservoir, and at a short break in the trees discloses the second dam, with a little stone bridge below it that carries the road from the east

*(Continued on page 40.)*

A FARM ON THE RIVER WYE

THE HEAD OF CAREG-DDU

## THE ELAN VALLEY. *(Continued from page 38.)*

to the west side of the narrow valley. A hair-pin bend and a sharp rise lead to a small parking place beside the Pen-y-Garog Dam, whose high sparkling cascade made a striking picture in this wild setting. I left my car and used my camera for an hour, subjects galore catching my eye in quick succession as I moved about on the steep side of the hill.

While threading my way through the Elan Valley I had noticed a remarkable difference between it and other glens containing reservoirs. Most of them had been heavily planted with conifers, but here the hillsides were so precipitous that such a development would have been impracticable and fortunately they had been left in their natural state. On resuming my journey I did pass a plantation of conifers on the left where the ground was less steep, but it was not large enough to mar the beauty of the scene; this plantation is situated at a point where the Craig-goch Dam is first sighted a long way up the valley.

The road climbs higher up the hillside, with a few scattered trees between it and the long stretch of water below. As I progressed, the third dam seemed to be wedged tightly in a deep cleft between the hills, and when I reached it I turned my car and lunched before continuing my explorations. An hour later I scaled a hill to the west of the dam and from here was able to get a good view of the dam itself and of the long reaches of the highest sheet of water beyond it. The dam is set in bleak surroundings; low, green, rounded hills enclosing it completely. It is, however, a most desirable venue for those who wish to walk alone in peace, solitude, and contemplation.

The road continues northwards to Pont-ar-Elan, and there joins the thoroughfare that connects Rhayader with Aberystwyth by way of the Devil's Bridge. I did not traverse it because I was told the surface was very rough, and its passage perhaps too adventurous for a low-slung automobile. I returned by the way I had come in the late afternoon of this glorious April day, well satisfied with another splendid excursion into the sequestered heart of Wales.

Y FOEL FROM CAREG-DDU

THE VALVE TOWER, CAREG-DDU

PEN-Y-GAROG DAM

PEN-Y-GAROG

CRAIG-GÔCH DAM

45

# The Gower Peninsula

The Gower Peninsula lies to the west of Swansea; it is some fifteen miles in length and about six miles broad. Its gentle undulations are given up largely to cultivation, and the farmsteads with their white-washed cottages add considerable charm to the wide prospect. Three conspicuous eminences dominate the area: the ridge of Cefn-y-Bryn, rising to 610 feet, slightly south of its centre; Llanmadog Hill, attaining a height of 609 feet, at its north-west corner; and Rhossily Downs, crowned by the Beacon at 633 feet, standing at its western extremity overlooking the long graceful curve of Rhossily Bay.

Known also as the " Land of the Setting Sun," Gower possesses a remarkably fine coastline on its south side between the Mumbles on the east and Worms Head on the west. Picturesque limestone cliffs rise sheer from the sea and are interspersed with sandy bays, rocky coves, and, occasionally, sand dunes, while a number of pretty wooded valleys run inland. A more or less continuous path affords access for the walker, accommodation may be secured almost anywhere, bathing, boating, and fishing can be enjoyed from the beaches, and the climate is salubrious: surely there is no more inviting seaside district anywhere in the country?

Since Gower is so near to the great city of Swansea, it is natural that this attractive peninsula should have become the playground of its inhabitants. Many of them have built charming villas in places as far distant even as Caswell Bay, while the Mumbles has for years been the home of the town's élite. Inland there is a system of twisting but well-surfaced roads, so that those in possession of a car can easily get to their places of business in the city. The tourist is especially catered for by an efficient service of buses which connects every corner of the peninsula, while a railway provides access to its north-east side and electric trams run frequently to the Mumbles.

After my excursion to the Elan Valley I planned to drive down to Gower next day, leaving Brecon in the early morning so that I could climb Carmarthen Van on the way. Unhappily some slight defect in my car delayed my departure for two hours, which made my arrival at Blaenau so late that I had to abandon the ascent. In the afternoon, therefore, I drove in leisurely fashion southwards down Nant Tywyii to traverse the long industrial valley leading to Swansea. Hundreds of dwellings flanked the road where children played carelessly, and a depressing atmosphere of gloom was every-

where. I passed through the war-scarred city, glad to have left behind all this desolation, and continued along the broad, curving road that skirts the graceful coastline of Swansea Bay and leads ultimately to the Mumbles. I tried unsuccessfully to find accommodation there, but eventually obtained a bed at a fine hotel above Langland Bay. I garaged my car, had tea, and, as the evening was warm and sunny, went out to explore.

I turned my steps in the direction of Oystermouth Castle, a ruin clad in ivy and perched on an eminence overlooking Swansea Bay and the Mumbles. It was built on the site of the original castle, burnt down in 1287. Parts of it are fairly well preserved and a path goes along the top of the outer wall. Next I proceeded downhill to the shore and, turning to the right, followed the road round Mumbles Point. This breezy headland reveals two islets which can be reached on foot at the lowest tide, the far one carrying a lighthouse whose brilliant white beam is visible at a distance of fifteen miles.

I followed the well-made path westwards past Bracelet Bay and Limeslade Bay, where it rises over a little promontory before descending on the far side to disclose the whole semi-circle of Langland Bay with its residences at the eastern end and a golf course to the west. The tide was out and laid bare a level stretch of sand, girt with shingle and a belt of grotesque rocks on the east, together with a little promenade overlooked by regimented bathing huts, all newly painted for the coming season.

Next morning was cloudy, and thick haze obscured the Devon coast twenty miles away across the Bristol Channel; but a fresh north-west wind sprang up while I lunched; it broke up the grey sky and brought the sunshine, so I continued my walk westwards in the afternoon. I kept to the twisting path which follows the coastline and is perhaps 70 or 80 feet above the sea, enjoying the changing vista as I advanced. Few people were about to revel in the glorious tang of the breeze, the shimmering sea, or the fantastic limestone cliffs which gave ample opportunities for my camera. The colouring was superb: a deep azure sea whose hurrying tides flecked the crests of the waves with white foam; gleaming yellowish white cliffs, ribbed, shattered, and riddled with caves; and above them a hillside decked with masses of golden gorse, russet bracken, purple violets, and innumerable star-like daisies.

*(Continued on page 50.)*

MUMBLES HEAD

LANGLAND BAY

48

THE SUNLIT SEA AT CASWELL BAY

Suddenly I turned the corner of Whiteshell Point, and there before me lay the graceful and lovely seascape of Caswell Bay. The receding tide had left the stretch of sand like glittering, polished glass, over which the seagulls soared and dived in the full glory of this April afternoon. I descended the path and climbed down the cliffs on to the sands, walking westwards across them to a small point adorned with pines. From here I had to scale the cliffs again to attain the path, and in circumventing the next headland, followed a risky course on the verge of the cliffs, where, looking down between my legs, I could perceive the sandy bed of the ocean.

Strolling along at my leisure in the invigorating breeze I came to Brandy Cove, a wild little inlet with traditions of smuggling. Skirting it, I crossed a stile, and then climbed round the next promontory which brought me to Pwll-du Bay, whose long line of cliffs culminate in a windy headland of red limestone. I sat down here for some time to enjoy the fine prospect while the sea broke into fine spray on the cliffs far below, and the sun dappled the restless ocean with myriads of diamonds. Eventually I returned to my hotel the way I had come, except that I took a short cut across the golf course where many players were enjoying an evening game.

I had invited Robert Tyssen-Gee to take his leave in my company and he motored down to join me that night. Next day was gloriously sunny, so we drove along the coast, leaving the car here and there as fancy dictated, and walked in search of beauty. We followed the sinuous highway to Bishopston and then made for Penmaen, where we parked our car. Going through a farm-yard, we took a winding path that led down to Three Cliffs Bay, a small inlet in the vast sweep of Oxwich Bay. We first walked over to the Great Tor, a pinnacled mass of limestone jutting out into the sea, and scrambled along its narrow crest, which in places dropped vertically for perhaps 200 feet to the sea far below. Retracing our steps, we skirted the cliffs to the east and with difficulty climbed down to the sands. The tide was out and we were afforded a magnificent view of the weird, isolated, leaning cliffs of Benwick soaring skywards and backed by Shire Combe in the far distance. Looking up to the left we could see the ruin of Penard Castle, high above the pebbly cove, and the numerous sandy tracks leading up to it.

We returned over the downs to our car and drove on to Port Eynon, passing the ridge of Cefn-y-Bryn on our right after leaving Nicholaston. The road drops sharply to the seaside hamlet whose thatched cottages, prim white houses, and quaint Ship Inn have made it a favourite with all visitors. We entered the bar of the inn to find almost every well-known brand of drink available, together with a galaxy of original flasks of famous liqueurs, most of which had long ago disappeared from the hotels of the large towns and cities. After a pleasant chat we drove on to Pitton.

We had been given to understand that this hamlet was a convenient place from which to explore Mewslade Bay, usually regarded as the most spectacular inlet in all Gower. We followed the grassy track through the trees, and then wended our way downhill to the rocky cove, which is shut in on either side by high, precipitous limestone cliffs. We sat down on the edge of the cove for some little time and then climbed upwards along the steep, well-marked track to the west. We scrambled along the knife-edge crest of every one of the wonderful cliffs which jut out into the sea, a steady head being necessary to avert disaster, for one slip would have incurred a fall of hundreds of feet on to the great boulders strewn along the shore far below. It was exhilarating work and gave ample scope for my camera. We made our way slowly along the full length of the indented rim of the bay, anxious to miss none of its grandeur, because it was the most magnificent piece of coastline we had seen. After spending two hours in this fascinating sport we returned to our car and drove on to Rhossily.

This village is the most westerly in Gower and is perched on the cliffs which frown upon the superb sweep of its sandy bay to the north. Leaving our car in a field, we walked southwards along the smooth green turf, high above the glittering sea, and made for Worms Head. Arriving at the Coastguard Station, we found the tide coming in and already engulfing the rocks which have to be crossed to reach the headland further to the west. The luminous ocean stretching away to the dim horizon threw into silhouette the weird form of Worms Head, which marks the western terminus of the Gower Peninsula. After a short rest we strolled back to Rhossily, where we partook of a sumptuous tea in a charming little garden overlooking the fine bay. We then, in the glow of a wonderful evening, drove back to Langland Bay by way of Oxwich. Both of us had been most impressed by the grandeur of the wild cliff scenery, and I am convinced that those who decide to follow in our footseps will enjoy every moment of their sojourn in the " Land of the Setting Sun."

CASWELL BAY

BRANDY COVE

PWLL DU HEAD

GREAT TOR, THREE CLIFFS BAY

BENWICK, THREE CLIFFS BAY

55

PORT EYNON

56

ROCK HEADLAND OVERLOOKING MEWSLADE BAY

57

MEWSLADE BAY FROM THE CLIFFS

RHOSSILY

WORMS HEAD FROM RHOSSILY

THE GRACEFUL CURVE OF RHOSSILY BAY

# The Pembrokeshire Coast

The coastline of the south-western arm of Wales is famous for its beauty, and although the whole of it is garnished with towering headlands, sweeping bays and rocky coves, it is a matter of opinion as to which part of it is the most picturesque. I had not the time to explore it all, and therefore concentrated upon the most southerly section, between Tenby and Milford Haven, because it is usually considered to be the most spectacular.

On leaving Gower, my friend and I motored to Tenby by way of Carmarthen, where he left his car to be collected on the return journey. It was the Sunday before Easter and we expected every hotel in Tenby to be packed. On arrival we enquired at some of them, only to find our fears justified, but one that occupies a commanding position on the south side of the town was able to accommodate us until the Saturday, with the possibility of boarding us out over the week-end if we wished to prolong our stay. This was a pleasant surprise, and we lost no time in taking possession of our room.

Tenby occupies a remarkable situation and is probably unique in Britain. The houses have been built on a long, narrow promontory flanking the western side of Carmarthen Bay, and are perched on the top of indented limestone cliffs which, at full tide, are inaccessible on foot. Steep, twisting paths, interspersed with steps and built-out belvederes, afford convenient passage between them and the sands, which at low tide present an alluring picture for both pedestrian and bather.

Castle Hill stands at the extremity of the peninsula, with the north and south sands on either side of the headland. The little harbour lies in a well-protected position on the north, and St. Catherine's Isle, dominated by an old fort which has been adapted as a private residence, lies on the east, being alternately a peninsula and an island according to the tide. The old town is enclosed by high, turreted walls, which are in a fine state of preservation; a south-westerly gateway, locally known as the Five Arches, being one of its most prominent features. Caldey Island lies two and a half miles to the south of Tenby, but only half a mile from Giltar Point, a promontory near the village of Penally. The island is crowned by a conspicuous monastery, and passage to and from it can be made by motor-boat.

The day after our arrival was cloudless and very hot for April, an opalescent sky indicating haze. But the weather did not deter us in our wanderings, and we were soon on the road bound for Manorbier. This famous Castle occupies a commanding position on rising ground overlooking Manorbier Bay and is one of the finest in South Wales. It was originally built in the reign of Henry I by Gerald de Windsor, but little remains of the Norman structure, and the extensive ruin dates from the end of the thirteenth century. Part of it has been reconditioned and is now a private residence. We spent an hour exploring its environs, and then went on to Lydstep.

Lydstep is famous for its caverns, which are situated in Sprinkle Haven, half a mile to the south. Leaving our car on the hill, we crossed a stile where a path leads downwards through a narrow defile, then winds its way to a rocky cove, girt with towering cliffs, and finally gives access to the three small sandy bays of the Haven. The beaches shelve down rather steeply, so that at low tide only can a safe passage be found round the two wall-like promontories that enclose the more westerly coves. Morning light is essential for the portrayal of the striking cliff scenery, so that perfect coincidence of tide and sunshine are imperative for success. One hour too late will spell failure, with the risk of being unable to get back again, which in turn would lead inevitably to tragedy, because the cliffs are unscalable even by the expert rock-climber. We were lucky, since the tide was on the ebb, and within half an hour of our arrival afforded a safe passage round the projecting points.

The superb seascape appealed to me strongly, for here were immense opportunities for both eye and camera. On the east the cliffs are composed of grey limestone, and on the west of green and red sandstone. The most easterly cove is precipitous and shattered, its floor strewn heavily with boulders and seaweed, and its walls riddled with caves. Some of the caves penetrate deeply into the limestone, but gaps overhead admit shafts of light which permit of easy exploration.

Having edged our way carefully round the first mass of rock to the west, we were immediately attracted by a cave that completely pierced the second promontory. This cave formed a gigantic window which framed the conspicuous and precipitous point further to the west. We rounded the next wall of rock and advanced towards the cave with the object of examining its narrow, vertical opening. The tide below it, with its incessant ebb and flow, was difficult to negotiate, but by careful timing we were able to spring on to the rock staircase that led up to the entrance of the cave, whose remarkable situation and striking rock architecture were most impressive,

*(Continued on page 76.)*

LYDSTEP CAVERNS

TENBY HARBOUR AT LOW TIDE

THE TOWN WALLS OF TENBY

MANORBIER BAY FROM THE CASTLE

MANORBIER CASTLE FROM THE SOUTH

SPRINKLE HAVEN FROM THE EAST

SPRINKLE HAVEN FROM THE WEST

ST. GOVAN'S HEAD FROM ABOVE THE CHAPEL (*bottom left*)

HUNTSMAN'S LEAP

THE PEMBROKESHIRE COAST LOOKING EAS

SADDLE HEAD FROM THE STACK ROCKS

PEMBROKE CASTLE

CAREW CASTLE

while from it we could see the whole of Sprinkle Haven, backed by Lydstep Point. The tide was now on the turn, so we hurried back to the first cove, where we discovered dry seats on the rocks and there ate our lunch, captivated by the soft murmur of the sea and the superb engirdling cliffs. After lingering for an hour we climbed to the crest of the crags and then walked westwards along them, scrambling out on to the end of each narrow promontory on the way to obtain a bird's-eye view of the whole scene. We spent the afternoon in this fascinating sport and then returned to our hotel.

Rain fell next day, but on the day after a strong north-east wind brought sunshine and cloud. We were on our way early and travelled westwards by way of the delightful Stackpole Estate, subsequently proceeding south through Bosherston to St. Govan's Head. The latter is the most southerly point of Pembroke, and we parked our car at the end of the lane within three-quarters of a mile of it. The cliff scenery hereabouts is some of the grandest in the country, and the plateau above is covered with smooth green turf. Here windswept promontories drop sheer to the sea, except in one place, so that walkers must exercise the utmost caution in approaching their edges, especially in a gale.

The long line of cliffs extends for miles, and the sole weakness in it occurs immediately opposite the end of the lane. Here there is a narrow ravine with a sloping floor, and about halfway down it is a hermitage known as St. Govan's Chapel, which is wedged tightly between the sheer walls of limestone. The path actually passes through the building, which, according to tradition, was the retreat of Arthur's knight, Gawain. The chapel is tiny, its interior measuring 18 feet by 12 feet; it has a ridge roof and bell-cote. We wended our way downwards to this relic of past ages and, after going through it, walked down a rough path that ends at a wild cove girt with perpendicular cliffs containing several caves. This strange spot afforded a magnificent prospect to the east, where St. Govan's Head projected out to sea high above the sundering tides of the ocean, its shattered façade catching the far-flung spray as the waves beat upon its rocky shore.

We returned to the top of the cliffs and turned our steps westwards in search of the Huntsman's Leap. This is the second ravine west of that housing the chapel and is so narrow at its seaward end that, were it not for the steep grassy approach on either side, an athlete could leap across the abyss. It owes its name to the tradition that it was cleared by a sportsman, who, however, afterwards died of fright when contemplating his feat!

Having viewed these extraordinary phenomena, we returned to our car and drove round to the Stack Rocks some three miles further west. A lane leads due south from the highway and terminates within a stone's-throw of them. The Stacks are two lofty columns of limestone which erosion, over countless years, has separated from the main cliff; the eastern Stack is the smaller and more slender of the two, and both of them are the haunt of innumerable sea birds, mainly guillemots and razor-bills, which arrive in April and migrate in August. The long line of indented cliffs to the east, ending at Saddle Head in the far distance, makes a sublime seascape when viewed with these spectacular isolated pinnacles in the foreground.

Regretfully leaving behind this marvellous panorama of cliff and sea, we drove to Pembroke to see its Castle. It is a noble ruin and stands on a gigantic rock whose sides rise above the tidal waters of the Pembroke River which flows into Milford Haven. It was formerly one of the largest and strongest fortresses in the kingdom, and its curtain walls, protected by towers, follow the natural configuration of its foundations. It has been restored in recent years and the Henry VII Tower rebuilt. The most revealing view of the Castle is obtained from a hillock to the south-west.

Next we drove on to Carew to see its grand, ruined Castle, which stands just off the road and overlooks a creek of Milford Haven. The building is rectangular, with a round-fronted tower at each corner and a gate-house on the east front. At various points inside it flights of well-worn steps lead to the battlements. On the present occasion cows were its sole occupants. The original structure is believed to have been the residence of early British Princes, but it ceased to be inhabited shortly after 1689. Much of the present ruin was originally erected under the direction of Sir Rhys ap Thomas, affectionately known as " the Valiant Welshman," and the chief Welsh supporter of Henry VII, assisted by Sir John Perrott, who was supposed to be a natural son of Henry VIII. We spent an enjoyable and interesting hour wandering round this relic of the past glory of Wales and then returned to our hotel, well satisfied with the revelations of the day. Next morning we bade farewell to Tenby and, turning our car northwards, crossed the lovely Prescilly Hills on our way to Devil's Bridge and Plynlimon.

CAREW CASTLE.  THE STATE APARTMENTS FROM THE QUADRANGLE

# Plynlimon and the Devil's Bridge

Our Good Friday journey to Devil's Bridge was without incident. The day was hot and cloudless, but the south-east breeze brought dense haze, so that when we crossed the charming Prescilly Hills they were dimmed and formless, which made the appraisal of their real beauty impossible. After passing through Cardigan we followed the coast road high above the sea, dipped down to Aberayron, and stopped for lunch outside Aberystwyth.

As we drew near to this seaside town we noticed the hill of Pen Dinas, with what we assumed was a high slender chimney protruding from its summit. We parked the car at its foot and walked up to investigate. A close inspection of the tall stone column revealed no inscription, but we discovered afterwards that it had been erected to commemorate the Battle of Waterloo by a local squire who was present on the field as an officer. Although the summit of the hill is only 413 feet above sea level it is a good viewpoint and discloses fine vistas of the Rheidol and Ystwyth Valleys, with the conspicuous isolated pile of the National Library of Wales perched on an eminence at the back of the town.

We went on to Aberystwyth, which occupies a remarkable break in the long line of cliffs whose erosion was doubtless caused by the waters of the Rheidol. As we drove northwards along the fine promenade, four features caught my eye: the Castle ruins on the headland; the striking position of the University of Wales; the lovely curve of the bay overlooked by Marine Terrace; and the dominating position of Constitution Hill on the north. This eminence is 485 feet high and boasts a funicular railway. I walked up the stony track to its summit, where were unfolded extensive views in all directions, but the finest prospect was that to the south revealing the three charming bays in front of the town.

Leaving this crowded resort behind, we turned the car eastwards and drove up the twisting road to Devil's Bridge. The surface was in good condition and the gradients easy for a powerful automobile; the finest viewpoint *en route* was at a sharp corner some nine miles from the town, where long stretches of the Rheidol Valley could be seen far below. Fortunately we had been able to reserve rooms at the Hafod Hotel, which occupies one of the grandest positions in the whole of Britain; the place was packed, and the superbly situated terrace in front of it was thronged with tourists gazing in rapt admiration upon the magnificent prospect of the wooded Rheidol Valley at their feet.

After dinner the numerous guests forgathered in the spacious lounge for coffee, and, scanning their faces, I soon picked out four of them who were real lovers of the hills. The rest of them were obviously motorists and ordinary tourists, who, disdaining the effort necessary to rove at will over wild country, would doubtless prefer to look upon it from afar. Three of the elect were ladies, evidently great walkers capable of their twenty miles a day, but one of them was less experienced than the others, for she constantly complained of fatigue after the strenuous efforts of the day. The fourth was a slim middle-aged sage of sunburnt countenance, whose loping stride proclaimed years of hill-walking with a certainty of foot that comes only from long experience of mountainous country. My prognostications proved to be correct, for, on entering into conversation, all of them disclosed an intimate knowledge of the topography of Plynlimon and its satellites, and of much of the country north of the Dovey. They were especially fond of the Welsh hills and we soon became friends.

The day after our arrival was dull and rainy, but the dawn on the following morning was brilliant. By ten o'clock, however, a strong and bitterly cold north-west wind had brought great masses of cumulus which dulled the prospect. Our bedroom windows looked out over the intervening hills to Plynlimon and we could dimly perceive its vast moorland slopes drenched in sunlight and patterned with swiftly moving cloud shadows. This was the last day of my companion's leave and we therefore decided to climb this hill.

Plynlimon is one of the three dominating mountains of Wales, the others being Snowdon and Cader Idris. The summit of Pen Plynlimon Fawr is 2,469 feet above the sea, but since its environs are already lofty the mountain lacks the imposing appearance of many lesser hills. The vast plateau extends from south-west to north-east and consists of grit and shale overlaid with coarse grass and bog. Satirists describe it as a " sodden weariness." This great dome is the source of the rivers Severn, Wye and Rheidol, and its slopes also give birth to several less noteworthy streams. It was Owen Glendower's lair in 1401, whence he sallied forth to harry the land.

There are two popular routes to the summit: that from the Dyffryn Castell Inn is the longer and traverses three and a half miles of a broad, gradually rising ridge; that from the hamlet of Eisteddfa Curig is about half

(*Continued on page 80.*)

THE DEVIL'S BRIDGE

the distance and threads a valley, to rise thereafter direct to the cairn at the summit. Both of them are well marked by a continuous line of stakes driven into the ground, which in mist are a sure guide, for they run right up to the top of the mountain.

We chose the shorter route, not because it was less arduous, but because I hoped the walk up the valley would offer greater opportunities for my camera. We drove round by Ponterwyd to avoid the ford on the shorter approach to Eisteddfa Curig, and emerged from gloom into sunlight about halfway there. The road rises gradually along a wide, desolate valley, but the monotony of the landscape is relieved here and there by a few larches which, however, disappear all too soon. A little hamlet stands on the crest of the pass at the divide between the Wye headwaters flowing east and the Rheidol tributary, Afon Castell, flowing south-west. We parked the car in the farm-yard, where a notice-board clearly defines the route, and, after changing into nailed boots, set off to scale the mountain.

Our starting-point was at an elevation of 1,358 feet, so we had to ascend 1,111 feet only to reach the cairn. It turned out to be a pleasant walk, first by a disused cart-track that ran beside a playful stream with chattering cascades here and there and led to an abandoned lead mine where we took to the grassy hillside, which carried the continuous line of poles but a very indistinct track, and finally attained the summit. There was absolutely nothing to relieve the monotony of the landscape during the ascent; no trees to break the skyline, no colourful flowers to carpet our way, no birds to charm our ear and eye, just the green and brown of the grass and bog, with racing masses of cumulus to enliven the blue sky overhead. Of the reputed sodden ground we encountered none, but this was probably due to the long spell of dry weather that had preceded our ascent. We could, however, well imagine the route in such condition after a heavy downpour of rain.

The approach to the summit is indicated by some outcrops of rock, but they do not extend far and we were soon standing by the O.S. Triangulation Station scanning the vast panorama that stretched away to the dim horizon in all directions. The atmosphere was none too clear, but we could dimly perceive the Arans far away to the north, and the great bulk of Cader Idris on their left. The latter, however, was largely obliterated by the voluminous clouds forming on it. The wind was strong and bitterly cold, so we put on Balaclavas and more pull-overs. We found a sheep-fold that afforded some protection and there sat down to eat our sandwiches. While we were pleased enough with the success of our short climb, we were scarcely impressed by either the

mountain itself, which sloped down too gradually to suggest its true height, or by the clarity of the immense prospect. It took us one and a quarter hour to make the ascent and half an hour to walk down to our car.

On the return journey we stopped at Yspytty Cynfyn and strolled down the steep path to see the Parson's Bridge. It is situated in a savage little gorge through which the Rheidol flows down to the falls opposite the Devil's Bridge. The rocks are polished and worn into fantastic shapes, and the river, when in flood, must be a wonderful sight as it surges along its tortuous course.

The scenery above the Devil's Bridge is commonplace, and consists of swelling moorland, widely scattered trees and a few farmsteads. Below it, however, the narrow wooded valleys and the torrents that thread them are a delight to the eye, and the falls of the Mynach, together with those of the Rheidol on the opposite side of the valley, make a picture that is unique in this country. Although the road at the Devil's Bridge passes over the highest of the three bridges spanning a spectacular narrow gorge, they cannot be seen to advantage from the thoroughfare, nor can the falls of the Mynach, because they drop to the north so precipitously and are completely hidden by the wealth of trees cloaking both of the enclosing slopes.

In years past the owner of the adjacent hotel must have spent a considerable sum of money in constructing paths, hundreds of steps and numerous belvederes so that visitors could view these attractions in safety, and those who wish to see them must quite rightly pay a small fee to do so. The only people who are exempt are guests of the hotel, so that my companion and I made several tours of inspection.

The three bridges are an astonishing sight. The original, which is known as the Monk's Bridge, spans the gorge at about half its height. It is not known with certainty when it was built, but the monks of Strata Florida Abbey are supposed to have constructed it about 1087. If this supposition is correct Archbishop Baldwin may have passed over it when he visited the Abbey with Giraldus Cambrensis in 1188. Another theory is that it was erected by the Knights Templar in the twelfth century as a means of communication between their hospices in this district. The middle bridge was built at the expense of the county in 1753, and the new one, which is an ugly structure, in 1901.

The best coign of vantage for viewing the bridges is about halfway down the steps, to which access is obtained by passing through a turnstile on the south side of the road. It is, perhaps, unfortunate that the steep enclosing slopes of this wild defile are heavily canopied

(Continued on page 88.)

THE NARROW GORGE BELOW THE DEVIL'S BRIDGE

THE PRESCILLY HILLS FROM CRYMMYCH ARMS

ABERYSTWYTH FROM CONSTITUTION HILL

PARSON'S BRIDGE

THE RHEIDOL VALLEY LOOKING WEST

MYNACH FALLS

JACOB'S LADDER

**PLYNLIMON AND THE DEVIL'S BRIDGE.** *(Continued from page 80.)*

with trees, because their branches and foliage prevent a clear view of the structures. A stout railed platform at the bottom of the flight of steps allows of the close inspection of the Punch Bowl, a huge circular cavity in the rock, worn and polished by the water, and situated immediately above the narrow slit in the crags that carries the oldest bridge.

Visitors climb another long flight of steps and cross the road to enter the grounds to the north of the bridges, which may be seen at close quarters by descending some steps immediately to the left of the entrance. The main path descends at a gentle angle and is fringed with trees through which glimpses are caught occasionally of the Rheidol Valley to the west. Seats are provided at the

THE TERRACE AT THE DEVIL'S BRIDGE

best viewpoints for the contemplation of the scene in comfort. The path turns to the left along a spur and drops sharply, steps being provided to facilitate progress. The Falls of the Mynach are here revealed on the left and make a strangely beautiful picture between the wooded flanks of the hill. A further descent leads to Jacob's Ladder—a steep flight of 100 steps—near the bottom of which is a circular iron bridge giving access to the steps leading upwards beside the Falls of the Mynach. Seats have been placed among the trees on the right, and from here exquisite views of the Rheidol Falls far below and of the thickly wooded folds of the enclosing hills on the other side of the valley may be enjoyed.

89

THE ROAD TO EISTEDDFA CURIG

PLYNLIMON FROM EISTEDDFA CURIG

91

THE TRACK TO THE OLD LEAD MINE

92

# Tal-y-Llyn

My companion returned to camp on Easter Monday and his departure marked the end of the glorious April weather. I drove him down to Aberystwyth in the first flush of dawn and, although the sky was clear in the east, great banks of cloud were piling up over the distant seas. The glass was falling and the wind from the west presaged rain.

I returned to Devil's Bridge for breakfast and by ten o'clock the crowd of holiday-makers had begun to arrive. Fortunately the rain kept off until evening and they were thus able to enjoy the usual round of sight-seeing, although the landscape had lost much of its colourful charm. The barometer went down steadily and rain continued throughout the following day. I stayed on in the hope of sunshine next morning, because, if it came, I wished to exploit the lighting in an attempt to improve upon my previous photographs of the badly illuminated bridges. While I waited patiently a few gleams penetrated the heavy cloud-canopy soon after 10 a.m.: an hour later I left for Tal-y-Llyn.

Descending the twelve miles of twisting road to Aberystwyth, I skirted the flanks of the Rheidol Valley far below and passed from cold and gloom into warmth and sunlight before reaching the town. The place was packed with visitors, many of them scantily clad and revelling in the splendid weather on the coast. Turning my car to the north, I drove along the hilly road in the direction of Machynlleth, passing the enchanting Llyfnant Valley on the way. On a previous occasion I had explored this narrow glen, which terminates where the Pistyll-y-Llyn comes down the precipitous crags as a gleaming cataract 300 feet high.

On crossing the bridge spanning the River Dovey I turned westwards to follow the northern banks of the estuary as far as the delightfully situated port of Aberdovey. The estuary widens out a few miles beyond the village of Pennal, and at low tide discloses a vast stretch of sand threaded by the glittering river. Luckily the tide was coming in and the wooded bluffs that flank the estuary on the north provided many a charming picture, reminding one of the French Riviera. The railway runs in and out of tunnels below the road, and the local authorities have done well to make it as inconspicuous as possible and have also provided access to the shore at different points so that visitors may enjoy the varied prospects to advantage.

After many stops *en route* I entered Aberdovey and parked my car on the promenade which, strangely enough, was deserted. I then sallied forth to renew my acquaintance with this delightful town, which is built in terraces on the hill overlooking the estuary and, since it faces south and is sheltered from the north by the hills of Cefn Rhos, enjoys a mild and salubrious climate. Eventually I returned to a seat on the promenade, and, while I was contemplating the lovely scene, cirrus began to form rapidly and soon became so dense that the sun disappeared. Heavy clouds rolled up from the west, so I resumed my journey by way of Towyn and the Dysynni Valley with the prospect of more rain on the morrow.

Tal-y-Llyn lies at the head of a narrow glen and occupies one of the most beautiful situations I know. The shallow lake is just over a mile in length and enclosed on all sides by precipitous hills, riven with gullies, and frowned upon from the north by the rugged spurs of Cader Idris. There are two small hotels at its western end: one of them at the outflow of the lake and facing the ancient church; the other tucked away round the corner below the steep flanks of Craig Goch and having an uninterrupted view of the whole mountain scene. The valley is so narrow that there is barely room for the road to pass between the shore of the lake and the hillside. The highway bifurcates about a mile beyond it; the right branch going over to Corris by a steep pass; and the left one mounting the narrow confines of the ravine between Mynydd Moel, the eastern outpost of Cader Idris, and the shattered slopes of Craig-y-Llam, to lead ultimately to Dolgelly.

I had stayed at Tal-y-Llyn on several occasions, first with the Rowlands and then with the Hunters, both families having a high reputation for kindness and consideration to their guests. The inn has a quaint, beamed dining-room, hung with sides of fat bacon, where the guests dine *en famille*. There is a cosy bar, decorated with record catches of fish and displaying cases containing samples of almost every variety of fly. The place is, of course, patronised by the angler—not just the ordinary fisherman who always hopes to catch a bigger basket somewhere else, but by the connoisseur in fly-casting and spinning, who returns again and again to this haunt of the wily brown trout. The talk in the lounge of an evening bristles with fishing technique: "Is nylon better than gut?" "Does this fly attract the fish better than that?" and so *ad infinitum*. Of course, the stranger

*(Continued on page 100.)*

94

CADER IDRIS FROM THE BIRD ROCK

THE BIRD ROCK FROM THE SOUTH

THE BIRD ROCK FROM THE WEST

THE RIVER DOVEY

ABERDOVEY

may be bored by this mysterious jargon, just as he may be surfeited with the chatter of rock-climbing experts in some of the remote mountain inns, but I always admit my ignorance and seem anxious for knowledge of this fine art, so that I am received with equanimity into its most select circles.

I remember an amusing incident that took place at this inn. It occurred one September when a newcomer arrived complete with all the exclusive gear of the expert angler. The tackle looked as if it might be new, and from its owner's conversation that evening the experts were obviously dubious as to his skill and knowledge. When the gentleman went out next morning to fish with minnows, however, they knew their worst fears had been realised, and the visitor was so severely ostracised that he packed his bags and departed next day, no one being sorry to see him go!

Many romantic names are associated with Tal-y-Llyn. There are, for instance, Big Fish Bay, One Tree Bay and Donkey Point on the north shore; and Nursery Point, The Refuge and Agony Point on the opposite side. These familiar spots, together with the Wilderness and Kennedy's Drift, will recall happy memories to those readers who have rowed their boats out in the morning in all sorts of weather, their hopes buoyant with the thoughts of trout for dinner that evening.

Days of rain followed my arrival, and while they held up my wanderings temporarily, the fishermen rowed out on the lake in spite of the weather: they returned rather sodden, but seemed content with the number of rises. One morning I woke to find a sprinkling of snow on the high ridge of Cader, and the northerly wind veered round to the south that afternoon, breaking up the grey cloud canopy and bringing sunshine. This welcome change induced me to motor to the Bird Rock, six miles to the south-west, and reached by a rough mountain road.

Known also as Craig Aderyn, this striking eminence is conspicuous from the road to the north of Towyn and should be seen by everyone staying in the district. Climbers will be fascinated by its spectacular western façade of sheer rock, as well as by the steep broken ridge that rises on the south-west from the road to its summit. The hill is really a bold, terraced scarp of the grassy ridge that separates the Afon Fathew from the lower reaches of the Afon Dysynni. Its height is not given on the maps, but I should imagine its summit to be about 700 feet above the road. The rock is appropriately named, because it is the haunt of innumerable birds, among which the hawk and the cormorant are common.

It is one of the few inland breeding places of the latter. I had seen Craig Aderyn several times, but on the present occasion I examined it more minutely in order to get a better idea of its topography. I then scaled the ridge, and when about halfway up found an exposed stance that revealed a wonderful view of the precipitous upper cliffs, backed by Cader Idris some six miles away to the north-east. From this excellent vantage point Pen-y-Gader assumed a fine profile and completely dominated the skyline. The upper part of the ridge is grassy and interspersed with outcrops of rock, but after the recent rains it was very slippery and it was necessary to climb carefully. Eventually I stood by the tiny cairn on the summit which disclosed a fine panorama of the long line of hills to the north, as well as stretches of gleaming sea to the west.

Indifferent weather followed, and, although I walked round the lake daily to keep myself fit, I spent much of the time writing this account of my wanderings. There were two days of a bitterly cold east wind that roared down the narrow valley and churned up the surface of the lake, leaving a white margin of foam at each of the little bays. While the anglers did not much care for these conditions their enthusiasm never flagged. They fished the quieter waters at the head of the lake, wading far out in its shallow reaches, but they always returned with the same tale of woe—no big fish, no tiddlers, not even a rise! I confess to a sneaking admiration for these gentlemen whose patience knew no bounds, but one of them, who in his early days had been in the Klondike Gold Rush, did not participate so enthusiastically. He chose his fishing days with discrimination, and during the stretch of bad weather kept indoors to sleep away the afternoons by the fire in the lounge.

The persistent east winds brought haze, which was often so dense that the end of the lake and the pass above it were completely obscured. On two of these days the bright sunlight induced me to climb Cader Idris and the Arans, much against my better judgment, because conditions were not propitious for mountain photography. It was my sixth ascent of the former and my third of the latter.

I remained at Tal-y-Llyn for eight days, but, since I could not afford the time to stay longer, I regretfully packed my bags and left it all behind. After bidding *adieu* to mine hosts and their charming guests I made for Bala, and, on breasting the last rise of the pass, stopped my car for a moment to take one last look at this lovely scene, crowded with memories which I shall cherish for many a day.

TAL-Y-LLYN

# Cader Idris

Cader Idris is one of the three chief mountains of Wales and ranks second only to Snowdon in popularity. Its summit is 2,927 feet above sea level, and although 43 feet lower than the highest peak in Mid-Wales it completely dominates the district. Consisting of alternate strata of Felspathic trap and slate, it takes the form of a long high ridge and extends for some eight miles between Cross Foxes on the east and Arthog on the west. Its northern front is precipitous and girt with crags and is broken in one or two places only; of those gaps the scree slope carrying the Foxes' Path is the most noteworthy. Beneath the crags are ranges of foothills, and below these again lie the Mawddach Estuary and the town of Dolgelly. Several rugged spurs extend southwards from the ridge and give easy access to it from Tal-y-Llyn and the Dysynni Valley, but one of them bends eastwards to form a grand rocky cwm in the bosom of which, and at a height of 1,552 feet, rest the stygian waters of Llyn-y-Cau. This scene is frowned upon by the steep, riven crags of Craig-y-Cau, the whole forming one of the wildest mountain scenes in all Wales.

Cader Idris is the traditional " Chair " of Idris, a giant whom the old bardic writings represent as having been at once poet, astronomer and philosopher, and who, moreover, is alleged to have studied the stars from his rocky seat on the summit of the mountain. The chair is the gigantic hollow immediately to the north of Pen-y-Gader and is hemmed in on the east by the Foxes' Path, and on the west by the narrow, shattered ridge of Cyfwry. It cradles the lonely waters of Llyn-y-Gader.

The extraordinary popularity of the mountain is due in part to its accessibility and ease of ascent from all points, but more especially to the extensive panorama unfolded to the north from the entire length of its crest. This superiority of outlook is accounted for by its position in relation to that of the Mawddach Estuary and the valleys extending thence to Trawsfynydd Lake in the north and Bala Lake in the north-east. Cader Idris also discloses wide vistas of Cardigan Bay to the west, with glimpses of Barmouth far below. When the atmosphere is clear the whole of Snowdonia may be seen far away to the north beyond the intervening heights of the Harlech Dome, while Plynlimon may be perceived to the south crowning the swelling moorland horizon.

There are at least eight routes of ascent, three from each side of the ridge and one from each end of it, but the finest of them all is that from Tal-y-Llyn. This route first climbs steeply to Llyn-y-Cau and then skirts its precipitous southern escarpment to traverse the crest of Craig-y-Cau, rising finally direct to the summit cairn of Pen-y-Gader.

I have climbed Cader Idris many times: once with Gerald Lacey in mid-winter when a sprinkling of snow lay on the mountain; and several times either in solitary state or with companions such as Dick Balcomb or Norman Taylor in late autumn, when the russet hues of the vast landscape added immeasurably to its charm. Leaving my car on one occasion at Llyn Gwernan, I followed the Foxes' Path with Norman Taylor, but we were so enchanted by the solitude and wild beauty of Llyn-y-Gader that we drowsed away the hours on its banks and never completed the ascent. I have also walked the ridge to and from Gau Craig and climbed to the summit by way of Cwm-Amarch, but the latter makes a better route of descent direct to the lake for those staying at Tal-y-Llyn.

On this occasion I drove to the gates of the Idris property, which are situated about a mile above the lake, and parked my car in a bay off the road. Changing into nailed boots I shouldered my rucksack and cameras and commenced the ascent by strolling along a level path beneath an avenue of conifers. Then, crossing a stile, I climbed the twisting track that rises rapidly through the trees beside the stream coming down from Llyn-y-Cau. Swollen by the recent rains the stream was hurrying down to the sea, there to fulfil its destiny: first by evaporation, then by condensation as cloud perhaps huddling round the high peaks, and again to be precipitated as rain in the eternal cycle of the universe.

I was alone, and the music of the water charmed my ear as I strode steadily upwards, my way made yet more pleasant by a few violets and daisies that had taken root in the stony track. A sharp rocky bluff drops precipitously to the east of the stream and is shagged with conifers, the fresh green leaf of the deciduous larches contrasting strangely with the duller hues of the evergreens. The trees to the west are more scattered, but their shade was welcome on this hot April morning; however, in twenty minutes I had emerged from their leafy canopy, and instead of taking the shorter route that rises steeply through the bracken on the left, I continued ahead, crossed the stream, and then climbed its left bank to walk westwards in the shadow of the frowning cliffs of Cader.

*(Continued on page 106.)*

THE ASCENT BEGINS HERE

THE PRECIPICES OF CADER IDRIS FROM A HILL TO TH

YNYDD MOEL (*left*), PEN-Y-GADER (*centre*),—CYFWRY (*right*)

CWM-Y-CAU

CADER IDRIS. (*Continued from page 102.*)

This is not the usual route followed by pedestrians; there is no track and it involves a detour of perhaps a mile, but it has the advantage of revealing a complete frontal view of Cwm-y-Cau. I could now see the upper cliffs of Craig-y-Cau above the long boulder-strewn ridge that encloses the tarn hidden at its feet. It rose into the opalescent sky as a gigantic pyramid, with the detached obelisk of rock known as the Pencoed Pillar on its left, the sheer walls of the latter clearly defined by its shadow cast upon the façade of the main crag.

There is a steep pull up stony ground to the tarn, where a conspicuous boulder is poised beside the outflow. I did not climb direct to it, however, because a rocky eminence to the north discloses a more comprehensive view of the whole scene. On gaining the summit I sat down to contemplate the wild prospect. Craig-y-Cau rose superbly on the other side of the black, forbidding waters of the lake at my feet, while the veiled sunlight, in striking across the face of the great cliff, threw into relief the shattered front of buttresses, gullies and grassy terraces, all of the latter rising diagonally to the right to peter out well below the sky-line of the pyramid.

The rock on Craig-y-Cau is unsatisfactory as a climbing ground and in consequence few mountaineers visit it. There are three gullies, of which the Great Gully enclosed by Pencoed Pillar is the most fearsome. The face of this detached pinnacle affords the most difficult rock-climbing on the Cader *massif*.

In due course I walked down to the lake and, skirting its shore, directed my steps to the left, where I soon encountered the well-worn track that leads upwards to the crest of the precipices enclosing the cwm on the south and provides an easy walk with extensive views towards Tal-y-Llyn, whose glittering surface is perceived occasionally through gaps in the folds of the hills. On the other side of the ridge the stupendous riven front of Pen-y-Gader can be seen across the dark waters of the lonely tarn far below. I plodded along steadily until I came to the Pencoed Pillar, where I amused myself for a short time by scrambling about on the short escarpment leading out to it from the ridge. I then walked up to the cairn on Craig-y-Cau, where I sat down to enjoy the warm sunshine.

In the course of this lofty promenade I noticed a diminutive figure below who was following in my footsteps. Ten minutes afterwards he joined me and I discovered that he was a keen mountain photographer. He showed me his recently acquired Leica, of which he seemed justly proud. We walked down to the col that joins Craig-y-Cau to the main ridge of Cader, and here I pointed out the exit to the stone shoot which affords a rapid descent to the lake in bad weather. The track ultimately passes below the shattered cliffs of the pyramid and then skirts the tarn to join the popular route of ascent below it. Pen-y-Gader towered into the sky ahead of us, its sharp, rocky summit crowning the long

LLYN-Y-CAU

ridge which stretched away dimly to right and left. We parted at the col, my companion following the well-worn track to the cairn, while I took a northerly course in a direct line with Cyfwry that led me to the verge of the cliffs enclosing the cwm that cradles Llyn-y-Gader.

I walked along the stony crest of the precipices and soon trod the summit of Cyfwry. A backward glance from this belvedere reveals the most comprehensive aspect of the tremendous terraced cliffs of Cader, but on this occasion they were not seen at their best owing to the dense haze which completely enveloped the vast mountain scene. The Cyfwry Ridge is the occasional resort of the rock-climber, and although it is narrow above the conspicuous Table, which was once the scene of an accident to a well-known mountaineer, it consists of loose, unreliable rock and is best left alone. I climbed down a stretch of it, but was glad to return to the top again in safety.

Retracing my steps I skirted the edge of the cliffs all the way to the summit of Cader, which carries an O.S. Triangulation Station and, on clear days, discloses one of the most extensive panoramas in all Wales. There is plenty of shelter just below the cairn so that climbers can find a comfortable resting-place on cold and windy days.

Those who have been able to arrange for a car to meet them at Llyn Gwernan will descend the mountain by the Foxes' Path, which leaves the ridge some little

distance to the east of the summit. They will pass both Llyn-y-Gader and Llyn-y-Gafr on the way down and obtain remarkable retrospects of the long line of precipices in the late afternoon sunlight. Those who wish to return to Tal-y-Llyn, however, have four courses open to them: they can return the way they came, but may shorten the route by descending the stone shoot at the col; they can diverge to the right at this point and traverse the crest of Cwm-Amarch, walking thereafter down steep grass slopes past a little shimmering tarn direct to the lake; they can stroll eastwards along the first section of the ridge, but bear to the right before encountering Mynydd Moel and then go down a rather indistinct track beside a dilapidated stone wall to join the route of ascent immediately above the trees; and they can continue eastwards along the entire length of the summit ridge, traversing Mynydd Moel *en route*, and thereafter descend to the road near the crest of the pass. The latter is undoubtedly the finest walk, with the Arans prominent on the north-eastern sky-line all the way.

On this occasion I descended by the first route. The day had been the most disappointing of these wanderings, but since I already possessed a fairly complete set of photographs of Cader Idris, many of which are reproduced here, I took a philosophical view of it. I had, however, enjoyed the strenuous exercise and it gave me a splendid appetite for the sumptuous tea awaiting me at my hotel.

PEN-Y-GADER FROM CRAIG-Y-CAU

THE PRECIPICES OF PEN-Y-GADER—FOXES PATH ON THE LEFT

SNOWDON AND THE HARLECH DOME FROM CYFWRY

THE MAWDDACH ESTUARY FROM CYFWRY

MYNYDD MOEL FROM PEN-Y-GADER

TYRAU-MAWR FROM ABOVE LLYN-Y-GADER

# The Dolgelly District

Dolgelly is the county town of Merionethshire and a splendid centre for a number of attractive excursions. I did not stay there because I preferred the more sequestered inn at Tal-y-Llyn, but I visited it several times and explored the many beauty spots in the neighbourhood.

Those who have a car at their disposal should drive along the sinuous highway to Barmouth in the late afternoon, since it discloses many lovely prospects of the Mawddach Estuary, which is hemmed in by steep wooded bluffs on either side. If a day is selected when a glorious sunset coincides with a high tide, the marvellous pageantry of the heavens will be reflected by the gleaming stretches of water, and the scene will more than repay the effort needed to see it.

At Llanellwyd Bridge the road passes near the remains of Cymmer Abbey, a Cistercian foundation dating from about A.D. 1200.

The Torrent Walk is a favourite excursion and follows the banks of the turbulent Clywedog, which descends a rocky gorge almost parallel with a section of the road to Tal-y-Llyn. The best way to see the water-play of the numerous falls and cataracts is to wander uphill beside it, access being gained by a wicket-gate at its lower end. The trees are festooned with mosses and lichens, a sure sign of a humid atmosphere, and the shafts of sunlight which penetrate them, and at the same time impart a glitter to the water, make the outing a delight to the eye, while the stream provides sweet music for the ear.

The Precipice Walk is the *pièce de résistance* of the neighbourhood. I was so charmed with it on my first visit, when I meandered along its varied stretches with Norman Taylor, that I went there again alone to contemplate its beauty in solitude. The beginning of the walk is in a rather secluded spot and in consequence is difficult to locate. The best way to find it is to leave Dolgelly by the Bala road and to take the left branch at the first fork and pursue a narrow winding lane that follows the contours of the hillside and eventually passes a quaint cottage on the left. Those who come by car may park their vehicle in a side road near the cottage where a broken-down stile gives access to the fields on the right.

The path follows a wall, passes some farm buildings, climbs a little knoll and leads through the trees cloaking the side of the hill. One or two stiles are crossed and then a turn to the left brings into view ahead the shining water of Llyn Cynwch. This tarn lies at a height of 1,068 feet and reveals a fine retrospect of Cader Idris across the valley to the south.

A grassy path skirts the western shore of Llyn Cynwch and, entering a coppice, wanders along the water's edge to emerge eventually near a fine group of lofty pines. This spot discloses a grand vista of Rhobell Fawr, and this mountain continues to feature as a prominent object to the north-east as the walker completes the circuit of a hill on the left. The views increase in loveliness throughout the advance, and when the refreshment hut is reached, at the most northerly point of the walk, the high ridges of Llawr Llech and Diphwys are sighted on the other side of the deep, wooded Ganllwyd Valley.

The hillside now becomes precipitous, and the narrow path threads dense masses of heather that cover the vast slopes on either side of it. Looking back from here the narrow glen can be seen far below, with the inn of Tyn-y-Groes wedged in beside the torrent that threads it. The western flanks of Cader Idris appear ahead, and the whole of this colossal mountain is revealed to advantage near the end of the walk, together with the long reaches of the Mawddach Estuary to the west.

The path makes a complete circuit of the hill and returns eventually to Llyn Cynwch, whence the car may be reached, but those who prefer to vary the descent may do so by walking down the broad grassy ridge at the southern end of Moel Cynwch. This route terminates in the vicinity of Cymmer Abbey.

Many visitors make Dolgelly their centre for the exploration of Cader Idris, whose spectacular walls overhang the town. The Foxes' Path is perhaps the most popular route of ascent, and the walk may be shortened considerably if transport is employed to Llyn Gwernan. The path favoured by pedestrians commences immediately opposite the hotel, but the pony-track begins at Dyffrydan, half a mile further along the road. The latter rises in an almost direct line to the Saddle, whence it bears east by a long line of cairns that terminate on the summit of Pen-y-Gader. The road above Llyn Gwernan continues in a south-westerly direction below the precipices of Cader as far as Tyrau Mawr and then bends away from them to descend to Capel Arthog. There are some revealing glimpses of Cyfwry on the way, and this ridge cuts the sky-line to the west of Pen-y-Gader, its profile assuming striking proportions and appearing almost vertical from this angle.

THE TORRENT WALK

CYMMER ABBEY

SUNSET ON THE MAWDDACH ESTUARY

LLYN CYNWCH

RHOBELL FAWR FROM THE PRECIPICE WALK

GANLLWYD FROM THE PRECIPICE WALK

THE DAM AT LAKE VYRNWY

# Lake Vyrnwy

Lake Vyrnwy is the largest sheet of water in Wales, being nearly five miles in length and about a mile in width. It is well known as the source of Liverpool's water supply, which is conveyed there by a system of tunnels seventy-five miles long.

This gigantic reservoir is cradled in a long valley to the south of the Berwyns, and receives its supplies from a watershed that covers an area of over 36 square miles, with its highest point at an altitude of 2,050 feet. Until 1888 the valley was a featureless bog threaded by a sluggish stream; the flanks of the hills closed in to a breadth of less than a quarter of a mile at its lower end and were joined by a broad rib of rock. On this ridge was built the colossal dam which now impounds the waters of the lake.

The dam is 1,172 feet long, 144 feet high from foundations to sill of overflow, 127 feet broad at its base and carries the road by a viaduct of thirty-one arches. The lake has an area of 1,121 acres, contains 13,125 million gallons of water when full, and the top level is 825 feet above O.D. The works were begun in 1881, and supplies were first turned on in Liverpool in 1892. The village of Llanwddyn, whose site was about one and a half miles above the dam, was engulfed by the construction of the reservoir, but was subsequently rebuilt as a model village lower down the valley. A large hotel overlooks the lake from a rocky bluff near its foot and is patronised largely by anglers who fish for trout in the shallower upper reaches of the reservoir.

The road which encircles the lake is nearly twelve miles in length and follows the shore, above which rise bands of conifers, millions of which were felled to pro-

vide pit-props during the recent war. The denuded areas, however, are being replanted.

Lake Vyrnwy may be reached from Bala by a wild mountain road that crosses the divide at a height of 1,641 feet, but motorists who have any respect for their cars will be well advised to avoid it and approach the reservoir from the south-east by way of either Llanfyllin or Llangadfan. I motored over from Tal-y-Llyn, but it involved a journey of seventy-six miles out and home. Unhappily conditions were not as good as I could have wished, for the east wind brought heavy cloud and haze, but I had to make the best of them in the circumstances as I could not find the time to go there again.

My route was first by way of Dinas Mawddwy and Mallwyd, then, leaving the main highway at Pen-y-bont, I followed the narrow, undulating road which, after many twists and turns, led eventually to Llanwddyn. I first sighted the huge dam during the descent of the steep hill to the east of the village, and on reaching it parked my car on the road below the hotel.

I was able to give two hours only to viewing the lake, and did not motor round it because the road was in poor condition owing to the heavy lorries which had passed over it throughout the war. I therefore spent the time in walking beneath the trees that fringe the northern shore, proceeding some distance beyond the tower that houses the intake. On returning I strolled over the viaduct and subsequently went back to Tal-y-Llyn by the way I had come, delighted with its lovely prospects of water, tree and mountain, and hoping to revisit it on a more propitious occasion.

THE VALVE TOWER, LAKE VYRNWY

THE SOUTHERN END OF LAKE VYRNWY

# The Arans

The rocky summit of Aran Mawddwy crowns the highest mountain ridge south of Snowdonia: it attains an altitude of 2,970 feet, and is thus 43 feet higher than Cader Idris; 60 feet higher than Pen-y-Fan, the dominating peak of the Brecon Beacons; and 501 feet higher than Plynlimon. The ridge is one and a half mile in length and Aran Mawddwy stands at the southern end of it, the northern outpost being Aran Benllyn, which is 2,901 feet above sea level and overlooks Bala Lake.

These hills do not present an inviting aspect when viewed from the south and west and appear merely to crown a vast area of billowy moorland. If, however, Aran Benllyn is seen from Bala Lake its precipitous eastern front is disclosed, and this alone will tempt the mountaineer to climb it. On closer inspection this line of black cliffs, flecked with white quartz and seamed with gullies, will be found to support almost the full length of the ridge. The only break is at its centre, where a grassy spur extends eastwards, its lower slopes cradling the circular tarn of Craiglyn Dyfi, which is the birthplace of the River Dovey.

Both of these tops may be reached easily from any point to the north, south or west of them, but their eastern flanks are not so accessible. Those who wish to climb them from this direction may do so by approaching Bwlch-y-Groes, and then turning westwards along one of the subsidiary valleys. The most interesting ascent, however, is that of Aran Mawddwy by way of the hamlet of Aber Cowarch, which lies a mile to the north of Dinas Mawddwy. Here a narrow farm road diverges to the left of the highway and rises sharply between the cottages. It threads a valley patterned with green fields and watered by the Afon Cowarch and, taking a north-westerly direction, ends at the farm of Cae Peris, which is situated immediately below the frowning cliffs of Craig Cowarch. A foot-bridge marks the commencement of the best route to Aran Mawddwy, and ascends over grass before joining the old peat track that rises gradually for over two miles and peters out in the bogs at the foot of Dyrysgol. The latter is an undulating, grassy spur extending eastwards from the reigning peak, and its crest is traversed to the base of the rough crags that rise directly to the cairn on its summit.

I had climbed this mountain on two previous occasions: the first time with Dick Balcomb, who is an en-thusiastic photographer and was so keen on his initiation to the Welsh hills that he insisted on carrying my rucksack; the second time alone.

On this occasion I motored over from Tal-y-Llyn, and can recommend this line of approach, because the pass that goes over the hills from Cross Foxes to Dinas Mawddwy is a fine one and reveals to advantage, by morning light, during its descent eastwards, the rugged, crag-girt cwms to the south. Turning to the left in the village, I drove slowly along the bumpy road to Aber Cowarch with the sparkling cascades of the Dyfi on my right. I have always had qualms about driving a large car over the narrow farm road that turns off to the left at this hamlet, for if another vehicle were encountered one of us would be compelled to back for perhaps a mile. However, my luck held, for I met nothing other than a herd of fat cattle and eventually emerged from the hedgerows on to the large rectangular strath which is threaded centrally by the rough cart road and ends at the farm of Cae Peris. The farm is beautifully situated: steep green hills engirdle it completely and are broken here and there by a few hollows, while to the west it is frowned upon by the black, forbidding cliffs of Craig Cowarch.

I stopped here for a moment and, descending from my car, mounted a hillock near by so that I could obtain a more comprehensive view of this peaceful valley. I had not gone far, however, when I was heralded by a lusty "Good morning" from the postman, who was making his rounds on a bicycle, but had dismounted in the road below on seeing me. He was a short, wiry Welshman of ruddy complexion, and when I spoke to him of the grandeur of the scene, he said that I ought to have his job in winter when I should probably change my views! In the course of our friendly chat he told me that the strath was common land and used by the farmers for grazing their cattle, but that in his opinion it would make an excellent site for a Youth Hostel, with which suggestion I entirely agreed. After he had departed to complete the delivery of his mail, I drove on towards the farmstead, and after turning my car round ready for the journey back parked it at the end of the strath.

The morning was sunny with a slight breeze from the north-east. There were signs of cumulus forming over the mountain-tops to the west, so I lost no time in

(Continued on page 126.)

ARAN BENLLYN FROM DYRYSGOL

changing into climbing boots and set off to ascend Aran Mawddwy.

The trees canopying the Afon Cowarch were now in full spring garb and their leaves shone like lamps in the bright sunlight, while the stream below them murmured contentedly as it hurried down to the sea. A line of trees marks the direction of the old peat track, but they disappear completely once the whole of it is disclosed ahead. This track rises at a gentle slope for over two miles; it is cushioned with springy turf and fringed with bright yellow sedges. I plodded steadily up-hill on this long grind, and, as I gained height, the floor of Hengwm receded with every step until the stream which threads it was nearly 2,000 feet below me at the end of the path. During this part of the ascent I often glanced into the two cwms on the other side of the valley, one of which is girt with crags and gullies. I had descended both of them on previous occasions in the hope that they would provide short cuts, but, like all digressions from the well-trodden paths, they involved more trying descents than were to be expected, so that on this occasion I planned to return the way I had come.

The peat track terminates in a maze of bogs, but a wire fence rises towards Dyrysgol and is a useful guide to it in mist. After a short rest and a cigarette I continued on my way refreshed, and crossing the fence at about half its height, bore to the right towards some outcrops of rock where a lonely little pool lies on the level end of the spur at a height of 2,397 feet. This point discloses, for the first time on this ascent, the shattered front of Aran Mawddwy to the west, together with the cliffs of Aran Benllyn above the grassy spur in the centre of the ridge, as well as Craiglyn Dyfi far below held firmly in the grip of the hillside by a bulge in the grassy slope.

Dyrysgol narrows considerably as it bends round the head of Hengwm, and at one spot, where a gully falls precipitously to the south, it is so narrow that the edge has given way. This coign of vantage is a good one for the appraisal of the shattered façade of Aran Mawddwy, riven with gullies and surmounted by a cairn which is clearly silhouetted against the sky. The gullies are reputed to be frequented by rock-climbing initiates, and after examining many of them I came to the conclusion that they would not attract the expert, because the courses did not appear to me to be continuous.

After an excellent lunch I continued my walk by tackling the broken rocks that rise to the first cairn. They are not difficult to negotiate, but those who wish to avoid most of them may do so by following a sheep-track to the left which ascends mainly over grass. Soon I was standing by this pile of stones that marks the southern extremity of the ridge and discloses the reigning peak half a mile to the north.

The summit-ridge is broad and strewn with boulders, and I meandered along it at my leisure finally to climb the steepish crags that dominate the ridge, and stand for the third time beside the O.S. Triangulation Station erected on top of the cairn. As I looked about me and scanned the distant hills, a long line of swelling cumulus extended right across the horizon from north-east to south-west and lent added beauty to the wild prospect. It was, however, dissipating rapidly as it drifted over the Rhinogs, whose serrated sky-line loomed dimly across the valley to the west. On their left the great bulk of Cader Idris slumbered peacefully in the heat haze, while visibility was limited to the north by the pointed outline of Arenig Fawr: Aran Benllyn, however, was more clearly revealed at the northern end of the ridge. Turning to the east, I looked down the precipices that fall to the little tarn far below, but beyond I could only just make out the receding ridges of the high Berwyns owing to the haze that dimmed the whole of this gigantic, swelling moorland plateau.

Taking off my climbing jacket I sat down with my back against a warm boulder and there drowsed away an hour. Not a sound disturbed my peaceful reverie except the occasional whisperings of the breeze in the gullies below. On a previous occasion pipits had chirped happily as they flitted from boulder to boulder, but now there were none of them to charm both eye and ear. Nor were there any wild flowers to carpet this wilderness, only brown grass strewn with black boulders as far as the eye could see.

After a refreshing rest amid this vast solitude I wended my way downhill by the same route, and it was fortunate that I did so, because the lighting and cloud were infinitely better in the late afternoon and enabled me to take some successful photographs. When approaching the bottom of Hengwm I encountered the farmer whose sheep graze on these hills, and he told me that, although many hikers visited the district in summer, in winter he and his neighbours had the whole valley to themselves.

In conclusion, I have one suggestion for those who employ a chauffeur. They should continue northwards along the ridge from Aran Mawddwy, and take in their stride Aran Benllyn on the way down to Llanwechllyn. Here they can pick up their car and so traverse the whole of this delightful ridge in a day with the minimum of effort.

CRAIG COWARCH

CWM COWARCH

CRAIGLYN DYFI FROM DYRYSGOL

THE GULLIED EASTERN FACE OF ARAN MAWDDWY

ARAN MAWDDWY FROM THE FIRST CAIRN ON THE RIDGE

131

THE RHINOGS FROM ARAN MAWDDWY

ARAN BENLLYN FROM ARAN MAWDDWY

133

# Bala

After leaving Tal-y-Llyn I motored to Bala, taking the short cut by the narrow road that passes above the Torrent Walk. The sun shone in all its glory as I proceeded up the valley of the Wnion, which is flanked on the east by the steep moorland slopes of the Arans, and on the west by the craggy foothills of Rhobell Fawr. After passing the edge of Llanwchllyn I soon caught glimpses of the rippling surface of Llyn Tegid through the trees that canopy the lakeside road, and eventually entered the small country town of Bala itself.

I unloaded my baggage at the large hotel near the Square in the main street; parts of the hotel are nearly two hundred years old, for a plaque on the wall of the building bears the date 1759. George Borrow stayed at this inn, and readers of *Wild Wales* may remember his account of the strong ale brewed there and the noble breakfast provided by Tom Jenkins. Indeed, a Victorian atmosphere pervaded the place, for on entering my room I found an old silver candlestick, complete with snuffer, and it was only the sight of the electric light that reminded me of modern times!

I took advantage of the fine weather that day by motoring over the Berwyns to see the famous Pistyll Rhaiadr.

On the following morning there was no change in the weather and, since I had already climbed Arenig Fawr on a previous occasion under similar conditions, I delayed my departure in the hope of more propitious circumstances. Meanwhile I walked several times by the lake, which is the chief glory of the district and the largest natural sheet of water in Wales. On one of these excursions I sat down on a seat by the new promenade to engage in conversation with an elderly gentleman who was evidently spending his retirement in these peaceful surroundings. It appeared he had been the station-master in Bala for many years, and he gave me an interesting account of the cheap trips run by his company in pre-war years. For six shillings travellers could then make the circuit of Mid-Wales by rail, stopping for an hour at Festiniog and Barmouth to enjoy the views. He obviously loved the district of his birth, although his father came from Norfolk; but he felt that the Welsh did not know how to advertise their grand scenery. As he said, they could make out bills well enough, but were unable to attract the visitors to pay them!

On one occasion I went along to see the Tomen-y-Bala, which is just off the road near the station. It is a small mound that was thrown up by the Normans and is now crowned by a single tree of fine proportions. I was unable to gain admission as the keeper of the keys was out, so that I did not ascend the spiral path to scan the lake and the valley of the Dee from its top.

On my fourth day in Bala the wind veered round to the north, a welcome change which the other guests in the hotel did not appreciate because it brought heavy cloud that obscured the sun. It soon cleared off the haze, however, and revealed the Arans and Cader Idris to the south across the lake for the first time during my visit. The cold wind was invigorating, and wishing to take advantage of it, I set off after breakfast to walk over to the Youth Hostel which is situated about two miles from the town and just off the wild road to Lake Vyrnwy. On arrival I asked permission of the warden to look round the place, which was spotlessly clean and very well kept. The original building was known as Rhiweadog, and dates from the sixth century, but the present one was erected in 1664. It is as strong as a fortress and the walls vary in thickness from six to fifteen feet. There is a charming court-yard outside the main building, and entrance to it is obtained through a gatehouse whose spacious portals are hung with a magnificent door studded with metal and of great age. This was one of the most romantically situated hostels I had seen, and the youths and maidens who stay there during their tramping holidays are indeed fortunate.

The wind backed to the north-east again and was accompanied by heavy cloud and haze; it roared through the valley and transformed the lake into an angry sea. However, after five days of patiently waiting for the light, my opportunity to climb Arenig Fawr came at last, so I packed my bags and left Bala for Harlech. This mountain is very accessible from the road between the two towns, and I therefore broke my journey to make the ascent.

During my sojourn in Bala the kindly folk at the hostelry did their best, within the limits imposed by austerity rationing, to emulate Tom Jenkins. Moreover, the chambermaid was amazingly active for her years, and in ministering to my needs surreptitiously placed in my room every conceivable guide-book to the district, as well as the most blood-curdling thrillers.

THE ARANS FROM BALA LAKE, EVENING

THE FOOT OF LAKE BALA

THE AFON TRYWERYN FROM BALA BRIDGE

# The Pistyll Rhaiadr

The Pistyll Rhaiadr has always been regarded as one of the seven wonders of Wales, and after viewing it for the first time on these wanderings I have come to the conclusion that not only is the praise lavished upon it well-merited but that it is the most picturesque waterfall I have seen in Britain. While it is variously stated to be 260 feet and 300 feet in height, this is no criterion of its real beauty; there are others in the country that are higher. Many of them, however, are enclosed by narrow ravines that hide their charms, and it is the superb placing of the Pistyll Rhaiadr, no less than its skein-like fall, which, in my view, gives it pre-eminence.

This fall of the Afon Disgynfa is situated in a remote valley immediately to the south of Moel Sych, the highest point of the Berwyns. A narrow but well-surfaced road threads this valley from the village of Llanrhaiadr ym-Mochnant to a farm below the cataract, but the main difficulty is to reach the village itself from any of the tourist centres. There is, however, a station on the Tanat Valley Railway that runs westward from Oswestry, but to reach it involves a walk of some six miles. In these circumstances the seasoned hill-walker will do better to stay at Llandrillo, and from there climb the high moorland plateau to Moel Sych, thence descending to Tan-y-Pistyll by way of the secluded tarn of Llyn Llyncaws, and thereafter following the path down beside the stream. The nearest popular motoring centre is Bala, whence a marvellously engineered mountain road crosses the Berwyns at a height of 1,638 feet and leads down to Llangynag; it continues to Pen-y-bont-fawr and from there reaches Llanrhaiadr by a narrow twisting road.

After making exhaustive enquiries in Bala as to the condition of this wild highway (the first five miles of which I learnt was bad), I decided to risk the journey and left the town before noon on the morning of my arrival. After driving to the foot of Llyn Tegid I crossed the bridge over the Dee and turned to the left, but was careful to avoid the first unmarked fork on the right because it leads to the Youth Hostel, whence it goes over to Lake Vyrnwy by a rough mountain road which is now unfit for cars. Proceeding eastwards I took the right branch where the road bifurcates four miles from the town and at once noticed a rapid deterioration in its surface. It twisted and turned in hair-pin bends, and rose so steeply for about a mile that I had to exercise all my driving skill to ascend in

safety. One moment I was crossing a curling, stone bridge over a ravine, and a few minutes later was looking down upon it from the verge of the cliff two or three hundred feet above. The surface was much rougher than many of the mountain roads I had driven over in Wales, but after this sharp climb it was broad enough to allow two vehicles to pass one another easily.

After perhaps a mile of straight road I came to a gate, the only one on this route, and to my surprise an old man appeared suddenly from nowhere to open it. I put my hand in my pocket to extract a copper, but finding the smallest change was a shilling I gave it to him. He was so astonished and delighted that he continued to raise his cap until I was out of sight. The road surface beyond this gate is good and becomes even better after the divide of Milltir Cerig, which is marked by a stone at 1,638 feet O.D. I stopped here for a few moments to scan the vast moorland plateau, which was thickly covered with deep heather and sedge. Cloud was forming in the valleys to the east of it and the atmosphere became more opalescent as I drove down the pass.

This was unfortunate, because the road soon traversed the steep face of a hill on my left high above the valley watered by the Afon Eiarth, and the haze prevented the appraisal of its wild grandeur. This section of the road is about three miles in length and a masterpiece of engineering skill: in fact, it reminded me of many parts of the *Route des Alpes*, over which I have often driven from Cannes to Geneva.

The highway is level beyond Llangynag but the three miles between Pen-y-bont-fawr and Llanrhaiadr, which are shown on the map as straight, are the most sinuous and treacherous I have seen in Wales. I drove very slowly along this narrow stretch, keeping my eyes glued on every bend, and it was lucky I was so alert, because at one of them I met a small car driven at too fast a pace for such a road; the driver had to cut into the hedge in order to avoid me, but passed on undaunted.

Dropping down the steep hill to the little village of Llanrhaiadr I crossed the bridge over the river and, turning to the left between the houses, drove along the four miles to Tan-y-Pistyll, which is situated at a height of 1,000 feet. The Pistyll Rhaiadr is stated to come into view soon after leaving the village, but although I carefully scanned the hillsides ahead I did not perceive it until I turned the last bend which reveals the small farm below it. The matchless beauty of the scene, so

*(Continued on page 140.)*

THE PISTYLL RHAIADR FROM BELOW THE FALL

A FARM IN THE BERWYNS

## THE PISTYLL RHAIADR. *(Continued from page 138.)*

suddenly unveiled before me, compelled me to halt awhile. I therefore left the car and climbed over a wall into a field below which gave a clearer view of it, and there I gazed in rapt admiration upon the foaming white ribbon set amid the most picturesque of wooded environs.

The sun shone in unclouded splendour and displayed the colourful prospect to perfection: an isolated mass of gleaming white cumulus drifted far away behind the crest of the cliff and, together with the deep sapphire sky, added immense charm to the whole scene. Eventually I tore myself away from it and drove on to the little farm, where I parked my car. Its situation is very lovely, for it stands on the brink of the stream below the fall and is canopied with tall pines that stretch up the hillside and crown the crags that precipitate the cascade. An iron bridge spans the stream below the fall and affords a clear view of the whole of it. Perhaps two-thirds of the way down there is a strange rock bridge, and, behind it, a vast rock basin that receives the main fall. The water then surges through the opening and descends to the base of the cliff as a spout or true pistyll. My visit followed a dry spring and in consequence there was only a moderate flow of water, but I should imagine the cataract had lost none of its beauty thereby, because when the Afon Disgynfa is in flood the tremendous volume of spray alone must make it impossible to approach near enough to view it in comfort.

I spent some time in climbing the cliffs on either side of the fall but could find no viewpoint with a superior outlook to that of the iron bridge. I then returned to the farm, where I entered into conversation with the lady who resides there, first by asking for a glass of water, which she willingly provided, and then by commenting upon the grace and loveliness of the Pistyll Rhaiadr. She said that to see its varied moods one had to live there throughout the year; that in winter it was often frozen and presented a wonderful sight with gigantic icicles nailed to the cliffs which gleamed like polished steel; but that the greatest volume of water came down in February, when the spray was flung over the house from morning to night and the roar of the cataract reverberated through the valley. Finally, she advised me to walk up through the woods to the crest of the cliffs because there were several beautiful cascades there worth seeing. I took her advice and was delighted with them. When I came down again and offered to pay the usual charge for parking my car in her yard she would not accept it, saying that the wonders of Nature should be viewed without charge by those who go in search of them. It transpired that this lady was an evacuee from Birmingham, and with a charming smile she asked me to sign her visitors' book. I had much pleasure in doing so, and after adding a note of my impressions of the place bade her farewell and left behind this enchanting scene. I turned my car homewards, and on reaching my previous vantage-point looked back to take one last glance at the Pistyll Rhaiadr. The sunlight, however, had now gone off the fall which, in the gloom, lost much of its scintillating beauty. I would therefore strongly advise those readers who propose to visit it to go there in the morning if they wish to view this magnificent scene at its best.

THE ROAD OVER THE BERWYNS

PISTYLL RHAIADR FROM THE ROAD

THE CASCADE ABOVE PISTYLL RHAIADR

# The Arenigs

The Arenigs are the two conspicuous hills domi-nating the barren stretches of moorland in the northern corner of Mid-Wales. Arenig Fawr is the higher and more shapely mass and attains an altitude of 2,800 feet above sea level, while Arenig Fach is a mere rounded hump on the heathery wilder-ness to the north of it, and is 2,264 feet high. Both of these mountains may be ascended easily from any direc-tion, but the latter is of no interest to the mountaineer. The former rises immediately to the south of Arenig Station, on the Great Western Railway, eight miles from Bala and thirteen and a half from Festiniog. Since the station is on the 1,000-foot contour, the ascent involves only 1,800 feet of climbing.

The most direct route lies up a wide grassy hollow sprinkled with scree, whence the undulating ridge leads straight to the broad backbone of the summit, which falls to the south-east where it is embellished with a number of strange little peaks. It affords a favourite descent for those who traverse the mountain on the way from Arenig Station to the village of Llanwchllyn, a dis-tance of eleven miles.

The only interesting and revealing ascent of Arenig Fawr involves a considerable detour to the south-east and skirts the shores of Llyn Arenig Fawr at a height of 1,326 feet. This lonely tarn lies immediately below a number of outcropping buttresses which are the occa-sional resort of the rock-climber. From the southern end of the lake a rough ridge leads to a grassy plateau that preludes the final slopes to the cairn on the summit of the mountain.

On a clear day the view from Arenig Fawr is very extensive owing to the isolated position of the peak : Snowdon dominates the numerous prominent peaks on the sky-line to the north-west; a glimpse of Bala Lake is disclosed to the south-east and is backed by the Ber-wyns; the twin peaks of the Arans appear almost due south, with Rhobell Fawr on their right, the latter being capped by the long cliff-line of Cader Idris; while the engirdling scene is completed to the south-west by the ridge of high hills whose serrated sky-line is crowned by Y-Llethr.

On this occasion I left Bala on a sunny May morning when the sky was sparsely flecked with cloud, although the strong wind from the east brought too much haze for my liking. Driving westwards along the highway I took the left fork about half a mile from the town. This is the old Arenig road; it has a good surface for the first three miles, but deteriorates rapidly after passing an iron gate that gives access to the open moor. The white walls of a number of tree-girt farmsteads afford some relief to the barren prospect, but these are left behind at the gate and a wilderness threaded until the few cot-tages clustered round Arenig station come into view. During the greater part of this journey Arenig Fawr rises ahead, but it disappears behind a craggy spur as one approaches the hamlet.

Parking my car near the station, I walked back along the rough road until I came to a corrugated iron build-ing on my right, and then passed through a gate on to the moor. I had climbed Arenig Fawr once before when I had taken a compass bearing on Llyn Arenig Fawr, but it had involved the crossing of an escarpment with a descent over boulders, scree and deep heather, hence on this occasion I chose the more circuitous but level route.

After following a rather indistinct sheep-track for half an hour, the glimmering surface of the tarn appeared ahead, with shattered buttresses frowning upon it from the west and a terraced façade of rock overhanging it on the south. There are a few scattered trees and one fine group of conifers near the railway, but they are all left behind when the moor is reached, so that the set-ting of the lake is extremely wild and desolate with no relief to its sombre scenery other than the brown grass and heather which stretch in all directions as far as the eye can see. An occasional ewe and its attendant lamb would appear from nowhere, to trot out of sight again as I approached. I walked along the boulder-strewn shore of the tarn until I came to its outflow, which is now dammed by a low stone wall where some piers are a reminder of its earlier conversion to a reservoir.

Continuing southwards I left the shore of the lake and made for a rough ridge that rises gently at first, and then more steeply where it skirts the terraced buttresses; it was here that I first felt the tremendous force of the wind. Luckily it was behind me and thus facilitated progress, but it was so boisterous that I found it almost impossible to stand still while taking a few photographs.

The summit of the mountain came into view to the west after I had topped the cliffs and, although it was still a mile away, I immediately noticed a strange differ-ence about it. At first I thought a group of climbers were standing beside the cairn, but as there was no sign of movement I speculated upon the changed silhouette,

*(Continued on page 148.)*

ARENIG FAWR FROM THE EAST

THE BUTTRESSES TO THE WEST OF LLYN ARENIG FAWR

THE TERRACED BUTTRESS ABOVE THE SOUTH END OF LLYN ARENIG FAWR

ARENIG FAWR FROM THE NORTH-WEST

## THE ARENIGS. (*Continued from page 144.*)

(*Continued from page 144.*)

since, on my last ascent, some seven months previously, there had been no objects on the sky-line other than the O.S. Triangulation Station and the familiar dilapidated wire fence.

The wind almost blew me across the grassy plateau to the foot of the ridge, and when I attained the crest the force of the gale became a hazard well known to those climbers who tread the high places. I took what cover I could find by keeping to the western flank of the ridge, but every time I passed a little col I was nearly swept off my feet. After a hard struggle I eventually reached the cairn and only then discovered the reason for the metamorphosis. My imaginary group of climbers proved to be a monument recently erected to commemorate the death of eight gallant Americans who crashed in their Flying Fortress on August 4th, 1943, their machine having collided with the rocks a few feet below the western side of the summit.

I found a sheltered spot with difficulty and there sat down to rest while cumulus raced past a few hundred feet overhead to be dissipated immediately in the warmer air on the other side of the ridge. Unhappily the haze was so dense that I could only perceive the indistinct outline of the Arans looming dimly to the south. All the other hills were completely obscured, but the sunlight glinted faintly on Llyn Tryweryn to the west. Half an hour later I began the boisterous descent, but once I had left the ridge behind and had entered the grassy hollow to the north, a welcome calm pervaded the atmosphere. I walked down to my car in three-quarters of an hour and encountered only two parties of wayfarers making the direct ascent of the mountain.

Continuing my journey westwards I regained the main road and drove over the desolate moorland in the direction of Festiniog. On a clear day the descent to this village discloses one of the finest mountain scenes in Wales, which is revealed in all its wild grandeur as one turns a corner on the 1,000-foot contour line. From this viewpoint the Moelwyns rise finely above a deep valley to the west, their serrated summits cutting across the sky-line like a titanic saw, while their riven flanks, buttresses and gullies sink down steeply to the green glen threaded by a glittering stream far below. I have not seen them from this angle under snow, but I can well imagine their presenting a magnificent picture of alpine splendour, even rivalling the wonderful prospect of the Snowdon group when observed at winter sunrise across the Capel Lakes.

On the present occasion these hills loomed dimly through the haze and thereby lost much of their charm, but I stopped the car for a moment to gaze upon the scene. It brought back happy memories, for I was now approaching Snowdonia, whose peaks I had climbed again and again during the past twenty-five years, sometimes in the sombre magnificence of spring or autumn, at others in the alpine glory of winter.

Proceeding downhill I drove through Festiniog and thence to the valley at its feet. Here the road winds for a long way through an avenue of trees whose fresh translucent leaves glittered like gold in the sunlight. Passing cottages here and there I soon encountered the estuary, but the tide was out and I looked across its blazing sands to the houses of pseudo-Italian Port Meirion perched on the opposite hillside. Then, on turning a corner, Harlech Castle was suddenly revealed a few miles away, its ruined battlements standing on a frowning cliff high above the ocean. I drove on towards it and half an hour later was unloading my car at the fine hotel that overlooks the famous golf links and the sea.

LLYN ARENIG FAWR FROM CRAIG YR HYRDDOD

MEMORIAL TABLET ON THE SUMMIT OF ARENIG FAWR

150

THE MOELWYNS FROM ABOVE FFESTINIOG

151

# The Rhinogs

A long line of hills extends from north to south almost parallel with the coast of Mid-Wales and is known as the Harlech Dome. Moel-Penoleu forms its northern outpost and overlooks Tremadoc Bay, while Llawr Llech stands at its southern end and frowns upon Barmouth Bay. Y Llethr dominates this chain at an altitude of 2,475 feet, but is only 13 feet higher than its neighbour, Diphwys. The two peaks, however, which appeal more strongly to the walker are Rhinog Fawr and Rhinog Fach, because the former reveals the whole of Snowdonia to the north, and both of them cradle a number of wildly situated tarns. These mountains are 2,362 feet and 2,333 feet high respectively, and are separated by the desolate pass of Bwlch Drws Ardudwy. Moreover, they are two of the most rugged hills in the country and are strewn with large boulders and scree which, to make matters worse for the pedestrian, are literally covered with waist-high heather.

Rhinog Fawr is easily ascended from the farm at the end of the narrow road beyond Llyn Cwm Bychan, which, with careful driving, may be reached by car from the village of Llanbedr situated on the main thoroughfare between Harlech and Barmouth. Rhinog Fach is most accessible from the farm of Maes-y-Garnedd, which stands at the head of the Nant Col Valley and in the centre of the vast amphitheatre formed by the two mountains. It may also be reached by car from the same village by driving over four miles of a narrow, twisting and gated road. Those who are able to arrange transport would do best to drive to the latter place early in the morning, climb and traverse the two peaks, having arranged for their car to meet them at the farm beyond Llyn Cwm Bychan in the evening. This comprehensive route discloses the finest scenery in the district, and includes Llyn Perfeddan, Llyn Hywel and Llyn-y-Bi during the ascent, and Llyn Du, Gloy-llyn and Llyn Cwm Bychan, as well as the Roman Steps, on the way down.

I first climbed Rhinog Fawr on a cloudless autumn day when I drove over from Tal-y-Llyn with Dick Balcomb. We deserted the highway at Llanbedr and followed the rough hill road that threads the delightful wooded Vale of Artro before parking the car at Dolwreiddiog. Proceeding on foot from this lonely farm, we glanced at the pretty little cascade which is canopied with trees at a corner of the road and, on mounting the next little eminence, sighted Llyn Cwm Bychan below.

This charming tarn is overhung by the rocks of Craig-y-Saeth to the south, and its outflow is fringed with trees. As we approached it the surface was still and faithfully mirrored the sunlit leaves of the trees, but as we wandered along the shore gusts of wind quickly destroyed this fleeting impression of beauty.

Arriving at the farm at the end of the road we turned to the right over a bridge and followed the track through a coppice, to emerge eventually on the craggy hillside. It was here that we first encountered the Roman Steps, which lead ultimately to Bwlch Tyddiad at a height of 1,294 feet. Wayfarers who do not keep a sharp lookout, however, may miss the longest and best stretch of the steps because the path keeps below them for some distance. It begins on the other side of a stone wall and lies immediately below the crags enclosing the south side of the narrow defile. According to tradition the steps were constructed by the Romans to facilitate ascent and descent by their sentries, but they are now ascribed to mediæval times.

On attaining the crest of the pass we looked down on the wide and featureless moor of Trawsfynydd, and then turned our attention to the ascent of Rhinog Fawr. The rugged spurs of the mountain overhang the pass, and those higher up are far too precipitous to be tackled with safety. We therefore retraced our steps until we found a weakness in the ramparts, and here began the toilsome ascent. We climbed beside a steep watercourse, which was hemmed in by large boulders covered with heather, but our progress was rather slow as we had to tread carefully in order to avoid spraining an ankle. After some three hundred feet of this trying work we edged round a big buttress to find ourselves overlooking Llyn Du. This desolate tarn occupies a striking situation on the north side of Rhinog Fawr and is surrounded on its south side by broken precipices which extend upwards almost to the top of the mountain. We scaled a ridge at the west corner of the tarn and eventually reached the two cairns which crown its summit. Unhappily dense haze completely obscured the distant view and all we could perceive were Rhinog Fach and Y Llethr to the south, backed by the dim outline of Cader Idris.

The sun was hot and the wind had died down, so we ate our lunch in comfort seated on the boulders below the higher of the two cairns. After resting for an hour we commenced the descent, and started by taking a

(*Continued on page 160.*)

THE ROMAN STEPS

Y LLETHR AND THE RHINOGS FROM THE EAST

CRAIG-Y-SAETH FROM THE FOOT OF LLYN CWM-BYCHAN

THE APPROACH TO THE ROMAN STEPS

LOOKING EAST FROM BWLCH TYDDIAD

LLYN DU

RHINOG FACH, Y LLETHR, AND DIPHWYS FROM RHINOG FAWR

159

direct line for the lake of Gloy-llyn, whose glittering surface lay far below. However, the thousands of insecurely perched boulders hidden by the deep heather forced us to make numerous detours, in consequence of which we were rather fatigued by the time we reached its shore. The lake is cradled in a shallow depression to the south-east of Craig-y-Saeth and, since it is a favourite with fishermen, there is a well-marked track leading to it from the farm in the valley. We thankfully trod this thin line through the boulders and heather and, on reaching the road, strolled back to our car.

I had been rather disappointed in Rhinog Fawr, not so much because of the undisclosed panorama of Snowdonia from its summit, but more especially because of its uninteresting topography. On this occasion, therefore, I decided to climb Rhinog Fach and approached the foot of the mountain by way of Nant Col. As I have said, the hill road that threads this valley to Maes-y-Garnedd is narrow and sinuous, but I had not expected to encounter so many gates. I did not count them during the four-mile drive there, but when I chatted with the farmer after parking my car in a grassy hollow above his home, he told me there were thirteen farms in the valley and that each one of them had its own gate! On the return journey I did in fact tot them up, but I could not make the total higher than nine; probably others had fallen to pieces.

I changed into nailed boots, shouldered my rucksack and cameras and, after being shown the way by the farmer, set off to climb Rhinog Fach. The sun shone gloriously in an almost cloudless sky, but there were a few patches of cumulus to the north driven relentlessly westwards by a terrific east wind. First I directed my steps towards a spur of Y Llethr because, from a distance, it seemed to be comparatively clear of loose boulders and heather. Finding I was not mistaken, I made good progress and soon came in sight of Llyn Perfeddan, which lies in a grassy hollow to the north of Y Llethr. I descended to it, because I thought it would provide foreground interest for a picture of Rhinog Fach, whose precipitous front towered into the sky to the north-east. The wind was less boisterous in this sheltered spot, so I was able to manipulate my camera more easily. A few sheep had been grazing near the shore when I arrived, but on seeing me they trotted out of sight among the boulders on the hillside.

Next, advancing in a direct line with my objective, I climbed a stony gully that petered out on the edge of Llyn Hywel, and it was here that I again felt the tremendous force of the wind. This tarn lies in a deep hollow between Y Llethr and Rhinog Fach and acted like a gigantic funnel, the wind sweeping over the col above it with the strength of a hurricane to churn up the surface of the lake in great waves and to throw spirals of spray in the air. It was utterly impossible to stand up in this wild cauldron of the Titans, but I struggled along the track, hanging on to boulders here and there, until I reached the calm at the outflow of the lake.

Looking around me the scene was grand and awe-inspiring: to the north the shattered façade of Rhinog Fach towered above the tarn; on the south the steep ridge of Y Llethr ran up to the sky-line, its sharp edge consisting of gigantic slabs of rock lying end-on at an angle of 45 degrees, and its base sinking down into the depths of the lake. Retracing my steps with difficulty, eventually I succeeded in reaching the south side of the tarn and there found a gully in the tremendous slabs of rock which I climbed to gain the wall running across the col. On the other side of it I could see the rippling surface of Llyn-y-Bi some distance below, but did not go down to it, preferring to take shelter behind the wall, where I rested for some time. Meanwhile the gale shrieked and howled in wild anger as it swept over the col, and looking down on Llyn Hywel from my lofty perch I could almost trace its course by the swiftly moving patterns on the blue surface of the water.

A track runs over all the summits of this long line of hills and I followed its course northwards on the lee side of the wall. The wall ends at the cairn on Rhinog Fach, but since haze obscured the fine panorama I did not linger there in the gale, preferring to fight my way along the bumpy ridge in the hope of soon finding a less boisterous route. However, when I came to the last small cairn the path petered out on the edge of a dizzy precipice overlooking Bwlch Drws Ardudwy. I climbed down the western face of this precipice, which was sheltered from the wind, until eventually I trod a little valley that led down to the pass. A heath fire must have raged there quite recently, for the heather was charred and the whole depression covered in soot; but I did not care, for I could now see where to tread safely, and finally emerged from it black to the knees.

Crossing a stone wall and then a brook, from which I drank copiously, I walked up to the path which threads Bwlch Drws Ardudwy and, turning my steps westwards, trudged over two miles of wild stretches to Maes-y-Garnedd, a remote farm that was the birthplace of Colonel Jones, a brother-in-law of Cromwell and one of the judges who condemned Charles I. Finally, leaving this desolate scene behind me, I drove slowly back, opening and shutting every one of the gates on the winding road, and not meeting another living person until I emerged on to the highway at Llanbedr.

RHINOG FACH FROM LLYN HYWEL

RHINOG FACH FROM THE SLABS OF Y LLETHR

Y LLETHR FROM ABOVE LLYN HYWEL

SNOWDONIA FROM MORFA HARLECH

# Harlech and the Lleyn Peninsula

Harlech is a pleasant little town perched on a hill 200 feet above the sea and is famous for its Castle, which stands aloof and unassailable on a bold rocky promontory, while its massive, towered, quadrangular walls afford splendid views of the mountains of Snowdonia rising beyond the sandy stretches of Tremadoc Bay to the north.

Harlech Castle was build by Edward I between 1280 and 1284, and its remains are admirably preserved by H.M. Office of Works, the imposing gate-house in particular being worthy of inspection from the airy promenade on top of the outer walls.

While thousands of tourists pay flying visits to Harlech to see this magnificent example of the past glory of Wales, those who stay there come to play golf on the Royal St. David's Links, which are laid out on the " morfa " or sea marsh between the Castle and the sand dunes. Since I did not expect to play this game during these wanderings I had brought no clubs and merely walked over the splendid fairways.

The celebrated panorama from the Castle walls includes the Lleyn Peninsula as well as Snowdonia, but those who wish to obtain an even better view of this extensive prospect should walk up to Moel Senigl, which is only 1,019 feet high and situated about two miles behind the town. It is reached by a steep road which starts immediately opposite the Castle, passes below this craggy belvedere and then meanders over the moors to Cwm Bychan. I strolled up to the cairn on the summit

of Moel Senigl one clear and cloudless morning, and was delighted with the magnificent panorama, which revealed not only Snowdonia, but also the Rhinogs, as well as Y Llethr and Diphwys to the south beyond the depression cradling Llyn Cwm Bychan.

My chief reason for staying in Harlech was to be near the Rhinogs, ascents of which I have recounted elsewhere in this volume. Since the fine weather continued I drove over to Nevin, which is situated on the west coast of the Lleyn Peninsula, stopping on the way to see such places as appealed to my fancy. The morning was sunny with traces of cirrus, which here and there paled the azure sky, but the strong wind continued to blow from the east as it had done for the past three weeks.

Proceeding in a northerly direction I crossed the toll-bridge in order to save eight miles of needless detour, and on reaching Minffordd took the left fork in the road, which leads through a long avenue of trees to Port Meirion. This remarkable retreat, situated on a private peninsula in the Tremadoc Estuary and surrounded by conifers and rhododendrons, is the creation and design of Mr. Clough Williams-Ellis. He has built an entire village in the Italian style, the gaily coloured houses and hotels being huddled together on the steep slopes beneath a slender campanile. It was unfortunate that the tide was out when I arrived, for had it been in flood the illusion would have been complete. Port Meirion is an ideal resort for the sophisticated visitor,

(*Continued on page 166.*)

164

PORT MEIRION

CRICCIETH CASTLE

HARLECH AND THE LLEYN PENINSULA. (*Continued from page 164.*)

who, in private surroundings, may indulge in every activity that goes to make a perfect seaside holiday.

The mundane dwellings of Portmadoc seemed incongruous after the gay little houses of Port Meirion and I was glad to leave them behind on my way to Criccieth. The great hills of Snowdonia form a vast amphitheatre round the green stretches of Traeth Mawr, but its conspicuous peaks disappeared one by one behind the low hills on my right as I drove westwards.

After a few miles of twisting road I passed over a hill and sighted Criccieth below me : it has a fine promenade that sweeps round the bay and is dominated by the ruins of the Castle, which was built or enlarged by Edward I and stands on a rocky promontory washed by the tides. I parked my car near by and walked up to inspect it, but, apart from the splendid panorama of hill and sea revealed by its fine position, the ruins are not very imposing when compared with those of Harlech Castle, seven miles distant across the bay.

I continued my journey westwards, and, on reaching Pwllheli, drove along its deserted promenade, but was glad to pass on to the lovely country of Lleyn, a peninsula famous for the Saints' Road, trodden, perhaps a thousand years ago, by the feet of strangers from every shore of the Irish Sea—pious pilgrims, missionaries and hostile invaders. Every church recalls some Celtic saint, and marks a stage upon the pilgrims' way to Bardsey, sometimes aptly described as the Iona of Wales. Here

the country was so beautiful that I drove slowly in order to see it. The hedgerows for miles were decked with golden gorse, and the wayside itself was covered with the waving fronds of wild chervil or cow parsley. The cottages, too, were enchanting, most of them whitewashed, and many of them thatched.

Eventually a sign-post pointed the way to Nevin, but, instead of going there, I went first to Morfa Nevin and parked my car at the end of the road near the golf course. These links occupy a splendid position and extend along the top of the cliffs high above the sea. The coastline hereabouts is indented with numerous little sandy bays, each of them possessing a few white-washed cottages which greatly enhance the prospect. The crowning glory of the view to the north, however, is the shapely outline of the Rivals, which completely dominate this part of Lleyn. Known in Wales as Yr Eifi, they form a *massif* of three peaks, the highest of which is only 1,849 feet; but they provide a magnificent background to the graceful sweep of the cliffs and slope down precipitously to the ocean on the west.

I spent an enjoyable hour meandering along the path on the edge of these cliffs. They were covered with golden gorse and afforded colourful contrasts to the subtle blues of both sky and sea. I then drove on to Nevin, a small fishing town perched on the cliffs, where a ravine gives access to the beach by way of a steep twisting road. Its situation is delightful, and in the

THE ENTRANCE TO HARLECH CASTLE

season attracts hosts of visitors, but the view of the Rivals is not so good as that from Morfa Nevin, two miles further to the west. I strolled away from the town and discovered an iron seat, thoughtfully placed on a good belvedere, where, with the lapping of the sea to provide soft music, I sat for a while alone before driving back to Harlech.

On my last day in Harlech I woke to find Snowdon cloaked in snow and curtained with a wild sky that presaged a further downfall. The hills at the back of the town looked black and forbidding, although the seascape was brilliantly sunny. In these circumstances I decided to drive south to Barmouth, in the hope of finding agreeable weather, and on arrival there I was not disappointed. The town and the mouth of the Mawddach Estuary were bathed in sunlight, whereas Cader Idris and the hills facing it on the north were canopied with heavy black clouds.

I parked my car on the quay overlooking the little harbour and noticed that the sailors were busy painting their craft in readiness for the coming season. I then strolled along the immense promenade, but found few visitors there to enjoy the lovely hot spring weather. It seemed a good opportunity to view the famous Panorama Walk, so I enquired the way from the first lady I met. After giving me precise directions, she remarked on my queer garb, and enquired whether I was a mountaineer. It transpired that she was a member of one of my

climbing clubs and she kindly invited me to lunch at her home. I accepted with much pleasure and afterwards she accompanied me on the short walk.

We ascended the twisting road for perhaps a mile and then turned off to the right to pass through a gap in the hills that leads to the platform which is the main viewpoint on the Panorama Walk. There is a craggy eminence some 200 yards to the west and, on walking up to it, I was surprised to discover that a cairn had been erected below it on the verge of the cliff about 500 feet above the sea.

Conditions were not propitious for viewing the panorama at its best, because not only were the hills steeped in gloom but the tide was out. I could, however, well imagine the beauty of the sunlit scene to the east with the tide in flood, when it would doubtless compare favourably with the best prospects in the country.

The Mawddach Estuary is disclosed in its entirety, wending its way eastwards into the hills about Dolgelly. It is hemmed in on either side by wooded bluffs and frowned upon from the north by Llawr Llech and Diphwys, and on the south by the long line of impending precipices of Cader Idris. The seaward aspect is enchanting, and unveils a bird's-eye view of the long railway bridge which spans the estuary with the houses of Fairbourne on the left and a few of the outlying dwellings of Barmouth perched on the cliffs on the right.

THE HILLS OF SNOWDONIA FROM HARLECH CASTL

OG (*left*), SNOWDON (*centre*), THE MOELWYNS (*right*)

PORTH NEVIN

THE RIVALS FROM MORFA NEVIN

PREPARING FOR THE SEASON AT BARMOUTH

CADER IDRIS AND THE MAWDDACH ESTUARY FROM THE PANORAMA WALK

# Craig-y-Bere

After nine days of perfect holiday weather I left Harlech and drove to Snowdonia, which is entered immediately after crossing the Afon Dwyryd. It was the clearest morning for three weeks, and on passing the Castle I could see the whole of Lleyn stretching away to the west beyond the glittering blue of Tremadoc Bay. The mountain scene to the north, however, was more fascinating and revealed the shapely cone of Snowdon framed perfectly between Moel Hebog on the west and the Moelwyns on the east. The dominating peak appeared much more imposing than usual because a fine cloud-pennant was forming on its crest and, trailing away to the south-west, cast swiftly moving shadows on the bare brown hills.

Although I had been climbing in this superb mountain district for a quarter of a century, there were still three of its ridges which I had not photographed to my satisfaction: Craig-y-Bere, the seamed precipitous front of Mynydd Mawr which is situated to the west of Llyn Cwellyn and overlooks the Nantle Valley; the Glyders, a fantastic rock ridge that rises between the Ogwen Valley on the north and the Pass of Llanberis on the south; and Yr Aran and the South Ridge of Snowdon which enclose Cwm-y-Llan on the east.

The day seemed perfect for the traverse of Craig-y-Bere, which in English means the Kite's Crag, and in the drive northwards to it all the hedgerows were decked with may blossom, whose honeyed fragrance powerfully scented the air. I first skirted the foothills of the Moelwyns, then passed the superb rock cone of Cnicht, and entered the narrow wooded defile of the Aberglaslyn Pass, to emerge finally in the green basin that cradles the charming village of Beddgelert. This village is an ideal centre for the energetic hill-walker, because it lies at the foot of Moel Hebog, is not far away from Cnicht and the Moelwyns and makes a good base for the exploration of the Snowdon *massif*.

Having crossed the stone bridge of the village, I turned to the left and ascended Nant Clogwyn, which carries the main road to Caernarvon. On reaching Rhyd-ddu I took the sharp hair-pin bend to the left, and, after driving along a mile of narrow hill road, parked my car on the crest of Bwlch-gyfelin. This pass lies at the head of the Nantle Valley and is hemmed in on the north by the ridges of Craig-y-Bere and on the south by the towering slabs of Y Garn II. Both of these hills are of about the same height and rise nearly 2,000 feet above the old copper mines which disfigure the upper reaches of the glen.

I set off by walking due north over the rugged declivities of Clogwyn-y-Gareg, which encloses the waters of Llyn-y-Dywarthen. After crossing its outflow I began a steady ascent of the grassy flanks of Mynydd Mawr, where a few cows, together with innumerable sheep and their lambs, were grazing on the luscious turf. My footsteps led me to the craggy spur that rises westwards to Craig-y-Bere and from here I could see Llyn Cwellyn down below on the right and caught a glimpse of the Snowdon Ranger Youth Hostel beyond. Another ten minutes of steeper climbing revealed the first prominent buttress of Craig-y-Bere on my left, and as I gained height others, too, came into sight. The best coign of vantage I could discover for the appraisal of this wild scene was just to the east of the summit of the façade, where a narrow escarpment of rock led out to the top of one of the buttresses.

I scrambled cautiously along its sensational crest to stand finally on this lofty sentinel. The scene was magnificent and awe-inspiring: the colossal front of Craig-y-Bere fell away at my feet and was broken up into precipitous buttresses of rotten red rock, many of them vertical, and all of them riven by gullies that descended from the crest of the mountain to the vast scree slopes beneath. Still further below and on the floor of the valley I could easily perceive the few cottages of Drws-y-Coed with the washing billowing out on the line, and then the ground rose sharply on the other side of the valley to terminate with the conspicuous tops of Y Garn II, Trum-y-Dysgyl and Mynydd Tal-y-mynydd, the latter carrying a lofty stone pillar, while the three together enclosed two impressive cwms. Looking to the west the sunlight glinted brilliantly on Llyn Nantle Uchaf, and far away to the south-west the Rivals and the sea completed the picture. Turning round I scanned the vast mountain scene to the east which was crowned by the pointed summit of Snowdon and supported by its graceful pendent ridges, of which that to the south with its prominent excrescence of Yr Aran looked the most beautiful. Beyond this superb display I could pick out the familiar tops of the Glyders, with the Carnedds on their left, while below me the broad valley tailed away in the direction of Beddgelert.

I climbed back on to the ridge where the fresh breeze was more invigorating and, after passing the summit, walked out on to each one of the spurs as I came to

SNOWDON FROM CRAIG-Y-BERE

them during my descent to the west. This side of the crag recedes a little so that it was impossible to see the whole of Snowdon from the tops of any of its buttresses; each one of them, however, disclosed the dominating summit, and while standing on one of them I noticed the black smoke of the train ascending from Llanberis.

I ate my lunch on the last of these airy buttresses, then walked down the steep scree slopes to Drwy-y-Coed and, after crossing the road, scaled the rocky outcrop which is a conspicuous feature of the north-western ridge of Y Garn II. It is only a few hundred feet above the valley, but sufficiently high to reveal Craig-y-Bere in its correct perspective. From there I walked across the grassy slopes to my car.

The afternoon was perfect, with a limpid atmosphere and fine clouds drifting to the south-west in a purple sky, so I drove down the Nantle Valley to look back on the wonderful prospect disclosed from the western end of Llyn Nantle Uchaf. The view is one of the finest in Snowdonia, for the crowning peak is perfectly framed between the precipitous flanks of Craig-y-Bere on the left and Y Garn II on the right. I had often gazed upon this scene, but I had never observed it in greater glory. Not content with this piece of good fortune I returned to Rhyd-ddu and continued on to Llyn Cwellyn and the Snowdon Ranger, which will be familiar to all readers of George Borrow's *Wild Wales.* It is now a fine Youth Hostel.

CNICHT FROM THE AFON GLASLYN

THE ABERGLASLYN PASS

THE MOELWYNS FROM THE AFON GLASGLYN

EVENING AT BEDDGELERT

CRAIG-Y-BERE FROM THE SLOPES OF Y GARN II

Y GARN II AND TRUM-Y-DDYSGL FROM CRAIG-Y-BERE

CRAIG-Y-BERE, SNOWDON, AND Y GARN II FROM LLYN NANTLE UCHAF

THE SNOWDON RANGER

# The Glyders

During my sojourn in Snowdonia I made my headquarters at Pen-y-Gwryd because it is well situated for the ascent of Snowdon and the Glyders, and is also a convenient centre for reaching the outlying groups of hills by car. The place is well known to all mountaineers and was for many years the home of the Lockwoods. Although I wanted two good days only for the expeditions needed to complete these wanderings, I had to stay there for a month to await suitable weather for them. During this time rain fell continuously for three weeks, which perhaps is not surprising, for it is the wettest district in Wales.

The Glyders rise immediately to the north of Pen-y-Gwryd and form a long undulating ridge that extends from Capel Curig in the east to Bethesda in the northwest. Their southern flanks are rugged but display no special features other than the shattered impending cliffs of Esgair Felen which overhang the Pass of Llanberis. Their northern front, however, presents a superb spectacle of wild mountain grandeur and is split up into several magnificent cwms by a number of spurs, of which Tryfan is the most striking, as it is one of the shapeliest mountains in Snowdonia.

The finest section of the ridge includes Glyder Fach, Castell-y-Gwynt and Glyder Fawr, the latter dominating the whole of it and attaining a height of 3,279 feet. The best way to see this spectacular rock scenery is to climb the rough ridge that rises to the south of Helyg, since from here one gets wonderful views of the three fine buttresses of Tryfan. The ridge peters out at Llyn Caseg-Fraith, whence Glyder Fach is reached by a long boulder-strewn slope that reveals grand prospects of Bristley Ridge on the right. From here the summit of the mountain is only a short step. Beyond it the main ridge is traversed in a westerly direction over the Castle of the Winds to Glyder Fawr, whence scree slopes lead down to the Devil's Kitchen, which is passed on the left; finally a broad shelf is descended to the mouth of the cavern, whence Ogwen Cottage is attained by one of the tracks round Llyn Idwal.

This is the most picturesque route and discloses the superb rock architecture of the *massif* to advantage, but it is not the most exciting. Those who wish to experience the thrill of height will ascend the North Ridge of Tryfan and, after walking down to the col on its south side, will scramble up the crags of Bristley Ridge. They will then traverse the main ridge as already described, but may shorten the route to Ogwen Cottage by descending Y Cribin, a narrow rock *arête* which is easier than it looks from the east.

Since I have already described and illustrated all these variations in other volumes, on this occasion I made the ascent of the Glyders direct from Pen-y-Gwryd and reached the ridge by way of the Miners' Track. The morning was sunny, but the east wind brought haze which dimmed the prospect of the engirdling hills. I set off across the fields behind Hafod-y-Gwynt, for there is no clearly defined track from the hotel, and made for the prominent stone wall half a mile away. The cairned path begins on the other side of it, and rises at a gentle angle as far as the rather boggy col: it discloses striking retrospects of Crib Goch and the Snowdon Horseshoe.

On reaching this spot I deserted the track and bore to the right until I came to the rippling waters of Llyn Caseg-Fraith, a charming little tarn cradled in a shallow grassy hollow. This shelf is a splendid viewpoint for Bristley Ridge, whose correct perspective, however, is better appraised from some outcrops of rock further to the north.

Turning my steps in the direction of Glyder Fach I walked up the long wilderness of boulders and scree until I passed the terminal rocks of Bristley Ridge, and then went over to the Cantilever. This is a long thin slab of rock poised on some erect boulders and will support a number of people without overbalancing. Many correspondents have sent me photographs of it, and one of them showed fifteen schoolboys sitting on its extremity.

The summit of Glyder Fach is near by and must surely be the strangest mountain-top in Britain, for it consists of immense boulders, chaotically arranged as a rough pyramid, and crowned with horizontal slabs. Castell-y-Gwynt lies a hundred yards to the west of it and is one of the most fantastic rock pinnacles in the country. It makes a superb foreground for the appraisal of Snowdon, whose conical top rises into the sky some four miles to the south-west. It consists of a mass of vertically arranged pointed rocks and is easily climbed on its north side, where sensational views are obtained down its precipitous face to Llyn Bochlwyd far below. Its western aspect is also most striking, especially when seen in retrospect from the track at the base of the crags.

Continuing my tramp westwards I passed the top of the Cribin and then skirted the edge of the Nameless Cwm, finally to attain the summit of Glyder Fawr, which dominates the whole ridge. Here is another

SNOWDON AND CRIB GOCH FROM PEN-Y-GWRYD GORGE

wilderness of isolated rock needles, but its topography is not so interesting as that of its neighbour, although its slightly superior height reveals a more extensive panorama. The vast solitudes of the Carnedds stretch away to the north as far as the eye can see on the other side of Nant Ffrancon and are crowned by the broad flat top of Carnedd Llewelyn. Snowdon and its satellites block the view to the south-west, while the Moel Siabod group of hills tails away to the south-east to terminate with the Moelwyns.

The Glyders are a popular venue with the ridge wanderer, and on the present occasion a number of them were sitting on Glyder Fawr to share with me the enjoyment of this wide prospect. The Devil's Kitchen lies immediately to the north and is reached by descending a long scree slope. While my companions followed this route, I walked down the south ridge of the mountain alone and in due course arrived at Pen-y-Pass, where I enjoyed an excellent tea in the back parlour of the inn.

PEN-Y-GWRYD AND HAFOD-Y-GWYNT FROM LLYN LOCKWOOD

SUNRISE AT LLYN LOCKWOOD

187

GLYDER FACH AND BRISTLEY RIDGE

THE CANTILEVER ON GLYDER FACH

189

CLIMBERS ON THE SPLINTERED SUMMIT OF GLYDER FACH

190

DESOLATION—GLYDER FACH FROM GLYDER FAWR

LLYN OGWEN AND LLYN BOCHLWYD FROM CASTELL-Y-GWYNT

CASTELL-Y-GWYNT FROM THE WEST

CAERNARVON CASTLE

# Caernarvon and Beaumaris

The Castles of Caernarvon and Beaumaris are within easy reach of Snowdonia, and I therefore took the opportunity of revisiting them during these wanderings. The former is certainly the finest in Wales and, with the possible exception of Alnwick Castle in Northumberland, perhaps the most magnificent in Great Britain. The erection of Caernarvon Castle was commenced by Edward I in 1283, and completed by his son. It was on two occasions unsuccessfully besieged by Owen Glendower. The structure was repaired in 1907, and further restored and strengthened in 1911. It was the scene, on July 13th, 1911, of the historic Investiture of the Prince of Wales, now Duke of Windsor.

I made three journeys to the castle from Pen-y-Gwryd before I had perfect conditions for its photography: the first time the tide was out; on the second occasion cloud dimmed its beauty; on the third I drove down to Bedd-gelert in the rain, and it was only on attaining the crest of the pass beyond Llyn Cwellyn that I noticed that the coast was bathed in sunlight. Caernarvon Castle is, of course, photographed by everyone, but it is doubtful if better conditions could ever be encountered for its successful portrayal than prevailed on this occasion.

Beaumaris is the capital of Anglesey, and to reach it involves a considerable journey from Pen-y-Gwryd. I went on there from Caernarvon, driving first to Bangor and then crossing the Menai Suspension Bridge, which was freed from toll in 1940. Turning to the right on reaching the island, I drove along the narrow walled road which reveals inviting glimpses of the Menai Straits through the trees, but on arriving at Beaumaris found the Castle closed and I had to do the best I could, in the circumstances, by photographing it from the green. It is a surprisingly low structure and was built by Edward I. The outer walls are nearly quadrangular, with round towers at each corner, but the inner fortress is surrounded by a moat, which in past ages was connected with the Straits by a canal.

THE MENAI BRIDGE

EVENING SUNLIGHT ON CAERNARVON

CAERNARVON CASTLE, THE WELL AND EAGLE TOWERS

197

BOAT REPAIRS AT CAERNARVON

198

BEAUMARIS CASTLE

# Snowdon by the South Ridge

The ascent of Snowdon is one of the ambitions of every hill-walker, and there are at least half a dozen fascinating routes by which he may climb it. Not one of them is very difficult under good conditions, and each reveals a different aspect of the peak. The least interesting is that followed by the railway from Llanberis; the finest that which involves the traverse of Crib Goch and Crib-y-Ddysgyl, the descent being made over Lliwedd, thus completing the circuit of the famous Horseshoe. The approach by way of Yr Aran and the South Ridge is perhaps the least frequented of them all, and it was by this route that I climbed to the lofty summit of Snowdon to bid farewell to the wonderful land of Wales.

Snowdon is 3,560 feet high and Yr Aran 2,451 feet above sea level. The latter forms a conspicuous excrescence on the long ridge running up from Beddgelert: it is a prominent object in the westward view from Llyn Gwynant, and in the eastward prospect also from the hills enclosing the Nantle Valley. Its north-western front is precipitous and displays a shattered front of rock; while its eastern spur, together with Bwlch Main, encloses the wild hollow of Cwm-y-Llan.

I left Pen-y-Gwryd on a clear but very cloudy morning, getting a lift down the four miles of road which thread the enchanting stretches of Nant Gwynant, and stepping off the vehicle at the pretty stone bridge which spans the Afon Glaslyn. Setting off along the familiar approach to the Watkin Path, I followed the right bank of the chattering stream that comes down from Cwm-y-Llan and passed the derelict mine workings on the way to Plas-cwm-y-Llan, where I found that the old house had been a military target, for it had been almost demolished by machine-gun fire. Thence I kept to the cart-track as far as the Gladstone Rock, which displays a tablet commemorating the opening of the Watkin Path by the famous statesman in 1892.

Turning away to the south I next ascended the grassy slopes that lead to the eastern spur of Yr Aran. The sky was clearing as I plodded steadily along the crest, and when I attained the peak at the end of the ridge the views to both east and west of it were exquisitely beautiful in the soft sunlight. From this angle Moel Siabod looked quite pointed and shapely in the north-east, where it stood high above the glittering surface of Llyn Gwynant, while the prospect to the west, which included Mynydd Mawr and Llyn Cwellyn, was especially clear

and lovely. Snowdon was still heavily canopied with cloud, and as its summit was obscured I sat down in the warm sunshine to await developments. I remained on this lofty viewpoint for two hours until conditions changed on Y Wyddfa, and then commenced the descent of the slaty slope to the col which separates Yr Aran from the South Ridge and Bwlch Main. There are a few small pools near Bwlch Cwm-y-Llan; each of them was still and reflected the glory of the sky as I passed on to attack the slopes of Snowdon.

The South Ridge is rugged; the crest slopes gently to the west, but on the east is hemmed in by precipices which drop down to the floor of Cwm-y-Llan. I made good progress up its steep acclivities, and as I walked gaily along the edge of the precipices I toyed with my camera here and there. Not a soul was in sight throughout the lower section of the ridge, but when I reached Bwlch Main I encountered several wayfarers descending the track that diverges to the west along the crest of Llechog. By this time the sky had almost cleared and no fine clouds adorned the blue dome above the lofty summit of Y Wyddfa.

The narrow path along the edge of Bwlch Main wends its way in and out of many bold outcrops of rock and discloses superlative views in all directions. The great hollow of Cwm Clogwyn lies far below to the west of it and cradles a number of small tarns which glittered in the sunlight. The vast solitudes of Cwm-y-Llan lie to the east, and the Watkin Path was conspicuous as a thin line on the steep back of Lliwedd. The vista above Bwlch-y-Saethau was particularly attractive on this occasion and revealed the Pinnacles of Crib Goch to perfection at the north-eastern terminus of the Horseshoe, as well as the noble summit of Moel Siabod, above which an isolated mass of cumulus slowly floated.

As I walked up the final slopes of Snowdon I could see the new hotel perched below the summit of the mountain at the end of the railway. It had been hot work climbing the South Ridge under an almost cloudless sky and I was glad to take some refreshment on reaching the hotel. Other belated travellers were there, awaiting the arrival of the last train to take them down to Llanberis. After a short rest I strolled up to the large cairn which crowns the summit of the mountain and there found a few climbers scanning the vast panorama of hill, moor and sea. The atmosphere was especially clear on this late evening, and in addition to all the familiar tops of Snowdonia, I

(*Continued on page 206.*)

THE SOUTH RIDGE OF SNOWDON FROM YR ARAN

YR ARAN FROM LLYN GWYNANT

MOEL SIABOD AND LLYN GWYNANT FROM YR ARAN

CRAIG-Y-BERE, MYNYDD MAWR, AND LLYN CWELLYN FROM YR ARAN

BWLCH MAIN

THE LAST CLIMBERS OF THE DAY ON SNOWDON CAIRN

SNOWDON BY THE SOUTH RIDGE. (*Continued from page 200.*)

could easily perceive the long line of precipices fronting Cader Idris far away to the south. Lliwedd cast an immense shadow across Cwm Dyli at my feet, where the waters of Llyn Llydaw looked black and forbidding in the increasing gloom. The crest of the northern half of the Horseshoe was still well illuminated, and Crib Goch stood out as a sharp little peak whose narrow rock *arête* ended with the conspicuous Pinnacles.

This was my last day on the Welsh hills, and, since I was in no hurry to get back to my hotel, I sat down on the shelf below the cairn to contemplate the beauty of the vast scene, and also to watch the relentlessly creeping shadow of the mountain as it grew larger and larger across Cwm Dyli as the sun sank lower and lower towards the horizon. I could hear the distant chug of the train as it climbed slowly above Clogwyn Du'r-arddu, and when it came level with the Zig-Zags the last few wayfarers on the cairn descended to the station to make sure of catching it down to Llanberis. Two other mountaineers remained behind, however, but they too left the summit a few minutes later and walked along its shoulder to descend the shaly track to Cwm-y-Llan.

I was now alone and, steeped in the mystic aura of the mountain, was able to muse in peace upon my recent happy experiences. I had spent four months in these wanderings and not only had seen much of the finest scenery in Wales, but also had climbed many of its prominent hills. Each one of these mountain-tops had had its own personality, so to speak, and although each had revealed a strangely dissimilar scene, that from Y Wyddfa was undoubtedly pre-eminent, not so much on account of its superior height, but more particularly by reason of the spectacular topography of its own pendent ridges. I could not count the number of times I had trodden its wonderful summit, but I had been there in all sorts of conditions ranging from the bitter cold of an impenetrable blizzard at Easter to the stifling heat of a still and hazy day in late summer. I heard the train depart, and after its loud screechings had died down on passing the gap above the Pyg Track, a strange silence crept over the evening and I realised for the first time that it was getting very late and that I must soon depart if I was to return to my hotel in time for a belated supper.

The sun was nearing the horizon as I commenced the descent by way of Carnedd Ugain, and when later I came to the Pinnacles I had to pick my way carefully over them in the gloom. I scrambled along the narrow ridge beyond and the only sound to disturb the impressive silence was the scrape of my boot-nails on the slippery rock. On reaching the small cairn on Crib Goch I lingered to watch the sunset, but as the sky was cloudless it lost much of its pageantry. Finally the fiery orb sank into the Atlantic away to the west and a strange chill stole over the atmosphere. I put on another pullover and started to climb down the long rock staircase which descends at an angle of 45 degrees to Bwlch Moch; it was tricky work in the half-light and needed care with every step.

In due course I reached the deserted col, and then trudged along the stony track down to Pen-y-Pass as the night was falling fast, so to end these fascinating wanderings through the heart of the fair land of Wales.

# INDEX

# INDEX